COLETTE BARON-REID

The best-selling author of *Remembering the Future* and *Messages from Spirit*

paths of choices   timeless town

of surprises

The Map

fields of dreams

village of victory

INSPIRATION MEADOW

Goblin nest

PORT OF LOVE

woodland house

soldiers of caring

THE FROZEN

GORGE OF GOOD AND PLENTY

COVE OF HIDDEN TREASURE

UNCHARTED LANDS

MAGIC STREAM

FINDING THE
Magic AND *Meaning*
IN THE STORY OF YOUR LIFE

Praise for *The Map*

"This book is wonderful, whimsical, inspiring, and revealing. It's the perfect read for those who have ever felt lost and unsure of where they are in their lives. It will empower anyone willing to enter a magical world where they can find their true destiny."

— **Courteney Cox**, star of ABC's *Cougar Town*

*"In **The Map**, Colette Baron-Reid leads you on an amazing journey of personal discovery. Her unique and magical approach will empower you in ways you never thought possible, revealing your unknown inner voices, helping you make better decisions, and guiding you to chart amazing new landscapes in your life. Immerse yourself in **The Map** and you will find that Spirit will lovingly assist you to create your very own Field of Dreams!"*

— **Sandra Anne Taylor,** the *New York Times* best-selling author of *Truth, Triumph, and Transformation*

*"In **The Map**, Colette Baron-Reid holds up a powerful mirror, revealing the commonality of experiences we all face in our efforts to find peace and purpose in our lives. This wonderfully effective tool for personal growth offers illuminating insight as to how we arrived at our current crossroads and how, by changing our perceptions of life, we can heal ourselves."*

— **Bruce H. Lipton, Ph.D.,** cell biologist; best-selling author of *The Biology of Belief* and co-author of *Spontaneous Evolution*

"In a language that's ancient yet familiar, Colette Baron-Reid shares intimate moments of true-life accounts and metaphoric scenery to remind us of the message that we are all connected to each other and to all of life. This is the book that you'll hand to your children with pride, while wishing someone had done the same for you in your quest to make sense of life's mysteries!"

— **Gregg Braden**, the *New York Times* best-selling author of *Fractal Time* and *The Divine Matrix*

The Map

ALSO BY COLETTE BARON-REID

BOOKS

Remembering the Future: *The Path to Recovering Intuition*

Messages from Spirit: *The Extraordinary Power of Oracles, Omens, and Signs*

AUDIO PROGRAMS

Journey Through the Chakras (music CD)

I Am/Grace* (music CD)

Magdalene's Garden* (music CD)

Messages from Spirit: *Exploring Your Connection to Divine Guidance* (4-CD set and guidebook)

CARD DECKS

The Wisdom of Avalon Oracle Cards

Wisdom of the Hidden Realms Oracle Cards

The Enchanted Map of You Oracle Cards
(available November 2011)

*All the above are available from Hay House
except items marked with an asterisk.

Please visit:
Hay House USA: **www.hayhouse.com**®
Hay House Australia: **www.hayhouse.com.au**
Hay House UK: **www.hayhouse.co.uk**
Hay House South Africa: **www.hayhouse.co.za**
Hay House India: **www.hayhouse.co.in**

The Map

FINDING the MAGIC and MEANING in the STORY of YOUR LIFE

COLETTE BARON-REID

HAY HOUSE, INC.
Carlsbad, California • New York City
London • Sydney • Johannesburg
Vancouver • Hong Kong • New Delhi

Published and distributed in the United States by: Hay House, Inc.: www
.hayhouse.com • *Published and distributed in Australia by:* Hay House
Australia Pty. Ltd.: www.hayhouse.com.au • *Published and distributed in the
United Kingdom by:* Hay House UK, Ltd.: www.hayhouse.co.uk • *Published and
distributed in the Republic of South Africa by:* Hay House SA (Pty), Ltd.: www
.hayhouse.co.za • *Distributed in Canada by:* Raincoast: www.raincoast.com •
Published in India by: Hay House Publishers India: www.hayhouse.co.in

Editorial supervision: Jill Kramer • *Project editor:* Alex Freemon
Design: Tricia Breidenthal

Library of Congress Cataloging-in-Publication Data

Baron-Reid, Colette.
  The Map : finding the magic and meaning in the story of your life / Colette
Baron-Reid. -- 1st ed.
     p. cm.
  Includes bibliographical references (p. 217).
  ISBN 978-1-4019-1244-4 (tradepaper : alk. paper) 1. Spiritual healing 2. Cog-
nitive maps (Psychology) 3. Magic--Psychological aspects. 4. Self-actualization
(Psychology)--Miscellanea. I. Title.
  BF1623.S63B37 2011
  131--dc22
                                2010035217

Tradepaper ISBN: 978-1-4019-1244-4
Digital ISBN: 978-1-4019-2949-7

14 13 12 11   4 3 2 1
1st edition, January 2011

Printed in the United States of America

This book is dedicated to all the remarkable people who have allowed me to "see" their magic, "read" their stories, and draw their maps.

CONTENTS

PART IV: MAKING THE MAGIC REAL

harbor

BY NANCY LEVIN

from this liminal state
we are reborn
into a threshold between worlds

through the fabric of fog
a map for another way
presents itself
we see—in a flash—how life
    could be

can we return to what is familiar
and make it new
finding mystery in comfort
or do we embark upon
the adventurous unearthing
together

surrender
to the acceleration of
    self-discovery
that can only come
from encouraging the emergence
of dormant forces
embracing this vantage point
let the past be memory

this pause
between present and future
is the alchemy
that will wake us
unlock us
transform us

there is barely a moment
even in morning twilight
when i forget
to remember
the shift is happening

i am a light in the harbor
leaving the weight
of the past at sea
change is my anchor
deep inside
peace is so close

FOREWORD

by Denise Linn

This morning, in the early hours, I finished reading Colette Baron-Reid's remarkable and moving book. I can still feel the wisdom of her words sinking deep into the core of my being. She majestically captures and describes the powerful forces that dictate the circumstances of our lives. This book also provides a map for each of us to discover new and vibrant pathways into the future.

Carrying the essence of her words with me, I climbed a tall hill to wait for the sunrise. In the stillness, I watched the darkness stealthily recede across misty valleys as the dawn light crept over the far eastern mountains. I love this landscape; whatever I look at—a lone oak tree silhouetted against the rising sun, the tall golden grasses bending in the morning wind, the jagged mountain ridge cutting into the red sky—tethers me to the earth. I feel my roots sinking deep into the soil, reminding me that I am but a sprout on the ancient root of my Native American ancestors. At the same time, this earthly haven for my roots allows my spirit to fly into the heavens, boldly reminding me that I am a part of what my forebears called *Great Mystery*. It is here that the soul listens to what the mind cannot hear. It is here that I'm called to remember the vast inner landscape of the soul that Colette so eloquently speaks about.

Most of us spend a lifetime trying to decipher the meaning of our lives. We search for it by examining the circumstances of our childhood, the obstacles we have faced, the hardships we have endured, and the triumphs we have experienced. We look for guidelines and spiritual systems to give us a strategy to maneuver through the convulsions of our lives in order to gain an understanding of the greater purpose of it all. We look for a map to provide a way to comprehend our past, guide our future, and allow us an awareness of how we fit into the larger picture.

In ancient times, the sacred maps that provided pathways through the generations of life had their source in the outer landscapes of the natural environment. The myths and stories of old that allowed people to understand their origins and where they belonged in the great cycle of life always had the backdrop of the natural world. However, these pathways into the deepest recesses of the soul have been lost, replaced with the modern chaotic speed of life that neither feeds the soul nor salves the heart.

At the same time that the natural environment is disappearing around us, we're losing vast tracts of the wilderness inside ourselves as well. The fertile soil of the soul is being gradually depleted as the songs of the birds are drowned out by traffic, and the scent of fragrant flowers is being replaced by exhaust. Something within us is dying as the chasm between humans and the natural world widens. We feel separate from the world around us and feel an increasing poverty of the heart and soul. It's time to find ways to remember who we are, and to rebuild the bridge back to an *ensouled* world.

For many years of my life, I took people out in nature on vision quests to recapture a profound connection to the earth. On these quests, people fulfilled their deep yearning for a viable connection to the mountains, the trees, the sea, the sky, and the sacredness of life. In the stillness of nature, people on their quest would experience a communion with the hallowed spaces within. These experiences in nature were powerfully and profoundly transformational. The energy of the natural world was indeed a catalyst for the hero's journey into the authentic self.

However, not everyone has the time or opportunity to embark on a vision quest in nature. Colette Baron-Reid, in her remarkable book, takes you on an inner vision quest that provides you with a mystical map with as much clarity and insight as spending time in quietude under the stars in nature. This book is a magical touchstone that allows you a profound understanding of the deepest forces of your essence. You embark on the hero's journey to identify the disowned, denied, or wounded parts of your being and then learn to integrate these aspects into your greater whole.

Colette shows you how to navigate within your own interior landscapes to hear the messages of the natural vistas that dwell inside you. The depth of the wisdom she has gained from the work she has done with thousands of people makes her uniquely qualified—perhaps more than anyone else in the world—to be the way-shower . . . and to be your spiritual guide for your journey ahead.

PREFACE

When I first began doing readings as a psychic/intuitive some 22 years ago, I quickly realized that to observe separate events in people's lives wouldn't be enough to help them. I'd see a major move, a job change, perhaps the name of a lover—all forms of events that the person had already experienced or would sometime in the future. Yet I knew that the real story was the internal process of how the individual came to meet that other person or find him- or herself in those particular circumstances.

It became clear to me that rather than focus on these separate events, it was more valuable to help clients envision a *map* of their lives. If I could show them where they had been, and how they got to where they were, the story of their lives would have greater depth and meaning, and they would have a deeper understanding of themselves. If I provided the unseen connecting elements of fate and destiny in what appeared to be unrelated experiences, I could empower people to make better decisions about their lives.

For that reason, I've come to think of myself as being a sort of "destiny cartographer" (*cartography* is the technique of making and drawing maps). So you might say I'm like a "life map" artist; I'm the one who, through my intuition, discovers the landscape of significant events in people's lives, then draws the finer details of the Map, which reveal their emotional and existential terrain. With that information, I can share a perspective that I hope will ignite something within them, some "Aha!" of understanding that they were unable to see until they were given the Map with which to find themselves.

When I provide this map, the person I'm reading is able to say, "Oh yes, now I see. That's where I've been, that's how I reacted, that's what I brought with me on my journey, and now here I am! Now I see the synchronicities and my part in them! I can create my destiny, not be subject to the whims of fate!" It reminds me of those giant puzzle maps I put together when I was young that spread across the whole dining-room table. Piece by piece, starting at the corners, I discovered how everything fit together.

I began to use the term *intuitive counseling* as a description of what I do because it evolved into more than just a psychic reading. My gift as a psychic allows me to see the events, the names, and the places visited that form the rough outline or chapter headings of my clients' lives. As an *intuitive counselor,* I look beyond the surface of things and into the intricacies behind people's stories: the motivations, unseen patterns, hidden agendas, and ancestral legacy. That's how the Map is drawn, and that's how it comes alive.

Of course, I had to learn the intricacies of this transformative mapmaking process for myself first. I had to navigate my way through my own story to find the hope, become the change, and discover the magic and meaning of it all. My own journey became the template for the process outlined in this book. I also drew upon what I learned from observing the stories of clients over 22 years and across 29 countries.

In other words, this book is based on experience, not theory.

This material is also rooted in *my* experiences. I've had to heal from many challenges in my own life, as described in my first book, *Remembering the Future: The Path to Recovering Intuition.* As a child of a Holocaust survivor who hid the truth about our family's heritage, I grew up with specific, peculiar survival issues that only made sense once my mother let the cat out of the bag that she'd raised us as Christians to be on the safe side . . . when we were really Jews. My wanting to be a Catholic nun when I was eight probably was more difficult for her to handle than I realized at the time. Looking back, I'd say we were colorfully confused.

As a psychic child, I was overwhelmed most of the time and had little capacity to understand healthy boundaries. Reality stretched into knowing secrets I wasn't supposed to, or knowing things that were about to happen that then did. Time and space were different for me than they were for others. That, and the suspicion of child sexual abuse by a babysitter, cast a distinct shadow on growing up "normal." Needless to say, fitting in wasn't ever going to be easy.

My teen years were difficult—no blame necessary, as my parents did the best they could. They were loving people who were perfect and flawed all at once. They had their own complex life stories that were influenced by *their* parents, whose stories in turn influenced mine.

My reactions to life were severe. I became bulimic at 14 and had my first alcoholic blackout at 15, which then escalated into a maelstrom of self-destruction and shame after a gang rape at 19. From the age of 19 through 27, I moved from one painful relationship to the next, where promiscuity, sexual abuse, violence, and drug and alcohol addiction were normal. I learned how to normalize trauma . . . and how to freebase cocaine. Only another recovering addict can really understand the gratitude I have today for the demoralizing way I ended up hitting bottom. I like to say that I took the express train to hell in order to have a true spiritual awakening.

January 2, 1986, was the day I woke up clean and sober—the urge to compulsively drink and do drugs mysteriously removed—and have remained so ever since. During the first couple years of my sobriety, I threw myself into 12-step recovery work and deep psychotherapy. I slowly began to claim my dignity and self-respect and surrendered to forgiveness. This surrender was crucial to my losing the victim consciousness that had become the motivating factor in my life up to that time.

Healing took quite a while, but I had a voracious appetite for learning and for understanding the psychology of how to heal; as well as what made me or anyone with my issues tick, why bad things happened to good people, and how good people could do bad things. I wanted to change more than I wanted to hold on to my old ideas. I also began to pursue my dream of a career as a singer-songwriter.

So while I was on the way to becoming a "rock star," Spirit had other plans for me. Frustrating, I know, but today I'm extremely grateful for the serendipity that brought me here. I began my accidental career as a psychic trying to make a living at my "day job" doing aromatherapy massage while waiting for my big break in the music business. Whenever I touched people, I would know things about them. I told them what I saw, and sooner than you could say "Shazam!" no one wanted a massage—they wanted a reading. I was failing miserably in my music career.

I didn't want to be a psychic, as I had a huge issue with that term and the stereotype. (Only recently, after 22 years, have I begun to own the word.) Plus, it didn't fit in with my vision of a sober singer-songwriter crooning about the meaning of life to masses of adoring fans. But it paid the bills, and I was deeply moved by my clients, so my career as a psychic (or as I chose to say then, "intuitive") took off like a rocket. Of course, the dream of being a singing sensation fizzled, although I did eventually sign a deal with EMI Music, to great critical acclaim and very limited success. Many lessons in humility learned.

As a psychic, I'm naturally very interested in the modern use of divination—the ancient, simple forms of spiritual inquiry common to indigenous people, as well as more complex systems such as the I Ching, Norse or Celtic runes, and the Tarot. All of these systems rely heavily on symbols and archetypes to tell stories about the human experience. Symbolism, archetypes, and metaphor have been used as a form of therapeutic language for guidance since the beginning of recorded history. I have created two very accurate symbol- and metaphor-based oracle systems, available as cards and computer applications, which are derived from ancient traditions. The use of metaphor as a tool for self-discovery is therefore one of the most important components of this book. *The Map* is essentially a metaphor for your life and all the territories, allies, and challengers you discover that are symbols of your deepest experiences.

Another important part of this book grew out of the personal work I did toward healing my wounded ego. Pioneering psychologist Carl Jung called this unhealed ego the *shadow*—it contains the parts of the self that we refuse, deny, or repress. Until I was able to name and accept the parts of me that identified with my wounds, I was unable to become the person I wanted to be.

Doing this painful work of self-examination and acknowledging these aspects of myself were the biggest hurdles for me, but they also brought me the greatest personal results. It inspired me to begin to look for evidence of the shadow in people's readings, and I saw how their patterns of suffering repeated when the shadow was denied. *Creating reality has much more to do with what is unseen and denied in the psyche than setting positive intentions.*

Enter the Goblin. I came up with this character during a guided meditation I was conducting that was supposed to introduce me to a mental form of my ego. The exercise was to help me see my "ego" as a strong, whole identity. In my meditation, I was to invite my "ego" to step forth to talk to me. I expected to see a vision of a slender, beautiful, confident, smart, slightly self-centered princess; and instead I got an ugly, smelly, Mr. Potato Head–like creature that sprouted hair, burped, and had a sign around its neck that said FAT.

I was so taken aback that I didn't know how to react, but instead followed the directions and invited this representation of my ego to talk to me. I received from this imaginary creature a litany of insults and criticism, shame, and blame that was startling. Then I noticed my favorite pink baby blanket, which I promptly wrapped around it. I cried my eyes out, realizing that I had to have a relationship with this being that characterized my wounding. The shadow had a form now: an ugly little Goblin.

Seeing this complex, self-sabotaging, active part of myself as a unique and separate character that was *outside of me*, and therefore not the whole me, was so powerful that it was like bypassing ten years of analytical therapy. A few years later, a friend introduced me to the process developed by psychologists Hal and Sidra Stone called *Voice Dialogue,* which I then studied further. From that, I considered, "Why not allow the Goblin to be the voice of the wound it was born of?" So I began to incorporate the Goblin character as a core element of my seminars and also offered it as a very specific coaching tool to help people separate from their inner critic to find a healthier, more neutral position within themselves.

It occurred to me that if there was a challenger within all of us, a voice we listen to that is negative, we must also have allies or more positive aspects to converse with as well, which led to the discovery of other characters with different attributes. This isn't a new concept, and my specific characters are derived from myths and fairy tales. Storytelling as a means of self-discovery is an essential part of my seminar material. We are our own fairy tales, all of us heroes on our life journeys. (Joseph Campbell's seminal work *The Hero with a Thousand Faces* greatly contributes to the concepts in this book.)

Eventually, I created an original process that combined elements of Hal and Sidra Stone's Voice Dialogue method with elements of an *active dreaming* technique, a powerful form of visualization that allows the imagination to describe the hidden subconscious patterns or stories that aren't readily available to the conscious, reasoning mind. This resulted in the creation of the In-Vizion® process, which all the exercises in this book are based upon. I've presented numerous seminars and weekend intensives in Sedona, Arizona, incorporating this material. I've witnessed true transformational and empowering shifts in virtually all of the participants.

Arguably the most important piece of this book came out of a question I asked myself while pondering the hero's-journey archetypes. If the hero has a thousand faces, and if he (who represents *us*) is on this adventure, wouldn't the hero travel through a thousand *places?* Could those places and environments be symbolic of where we live inside ourselves? What would it be like to turn away from centering on the self, from the position of an inner observer, and outward to symbolic sites that could tell us stories? Wouldn't it be true that since we've lost our connection to the outside environment, perhaps we might find our way back as we connect to our *inner* one as a living world we inhabit?

Earth-based religions and all aboriginal traditions value the planet as a living, conscious entity that we're in a sacred interdependent relationship with, rather than a ball of inanimate stuff we can use and dominate. My personal spiritual beliefs include revering nature as essential to connecting to a living, Divine consciousness. I believe all of us need to reclaim that sacred relationship to the natural world that surrounds us and that we're part of. That reconnection can happen *within* us, too, as we explore our inner landscapes: as above, so below; as outside, so inside.

And so we come full circle to the magic of mapmaking. If we can explore our lives as a journey through psycho-spiritual places instead of archetypal personas, our perspective changes drastically. Instead of always holding up a mirror to our faces, we look outside of ourselves in order to, paradoxically, find a deeper meaning for our lives. We also remind ourselves of the mystical and mysterious magic of the environment.

In my second book, *Messages from Spirit,* I wrote at length about how the natural world serves as an intuitive connector to the Divine. Oracles abound in nature, and as we develop a sacred relationship to all of life, we can begin to see and hear them.

Similarly, when we journey into the Map, we can find our own oracles and wisdom within our personal inner landscapes. Bypassing logic and reason and entering the magical world of intuition and imagination, we find empowering answers with respect to meaning, purpose, and hope.

The process and concepts outlined in this book are tried-and-true. All you have to do is step into the Map and let the magic reveal itself . . . as it reveals *you.*

May this book bring you wisdom, peace, and joy!

Love,
Colette

INTRODUCTION

Your Enchanted Map

Where are you right now? Close your eyes and describe where you *feel* you are. Are you in a Field of Dreams, where you're planting the seeds of your intention and are eager to see the results? Are you lost in a dry desert, where abundance eludes you? Are you wandering through the Valley of Loss?

This inner landscape may bear no resemblance to where you actually are located in time and space. You could be sitting in a sunny room, looking out at a beautiful harbor, but feel stuck in an unforgiving and harsh land that exists inside you. What you believe has a great influence on where you find yourself when you look within.

Do you believe that there could be more to life than you've come to expect, or are you filled with doubt because you don't know how to begin creating something better? Perhaps you think you're doing everything you can, but the results aren't what you hoped for; or you look around at the problems you see others facing and feel helpless to make their lives less stressful or painful.

Do you long for fulfillment, meaning—even magic?

My guess is that you're willing to work hard and do all the right things to get where you'd like to go: that glittering spot on the Map that beckons with promises of sanctuary, abundance, harmony, and serenity. However, a quick look at the path that brought you to this point will remind you that the journey is never as predictable or controllable as you'd like it to be. We could all use a little magic, couldn't we?

When I speak of magic in these pages, I don't mean the stuff of trickery, illusion, or manipulation that you see in a "magic show." The kind I'm referring to is the living evidence of the intelligent and dynamic mysterious essence from which all substance is created, shaped, and created again. The magic in this book is revealed to you through your very own capacity to perceive it and by your willingness to work with your imagination and with Spirit.

This magical energy has always been, is now, and forever will be. You can't understand it intellectually or analyze it logically, yet you can know it deeply at the level of heart and soul, through your intuition. This magic is creative and life bearing. It isn't something you can control, yet you can align with it and even swim beside it the way dolphins will mimic your movements as they follow alongside you in the ocean. If you're willing to enter into a partnership with Spirit and allow your imagination to be ignited and inspired, you'll be amazed by the results. You'll find your own personal connection to magic by stepping out of linear, left-brain thought, and entering the creative domain of intuition and imagination.

Why a metaphorical "map"? Symbolic language allows you to access the layers of experience that are stored in your subconscious mind and are often hidden from your everyday awareness. These are the beliefs and thoughts that determine what you're attracted to and what you manifest in your life. You decipher metaphors through your intuition, for it's the soul and not the mind that can comprehend their more accurate multilayered meaning. Metaphoric language allows you to move beyond the surface of things and enter a deeper reality.

Inside all of us are psychological landscapes created by our feelings and thoughts—the Storm Fields we inhabit when we feel like we're under attack, or the Sticky Swamp we become mired in when we're overwhelmed by our obligations.

If I ask, "Where are you?" you might instinctively respond, "Lost!" or "Trapped at the bottom of a deep pit," "Stuck in the mud," "Sinking in quicksand," or "Wandering through a barren no-man's-land." These images are far more powerful in describing the intensity and profundity of your experience than a mere list of your life's circumstances.

Once awakened to your inner landscape, you'll be able to consciously shape your world by altering that landscape within, rather than focusing on your external reality. Having caused the dark clouds within to depart, you'll discover that your inner sense of safety and calm is now mirrored in your outer circumstances. You'll also start to see the events in your life as part of a larger picture. This is when you find the real magic and meaning in the story of your life—and the bravery, strength, and wisdom to make empowered choices.

You Have a Map, and It Is Magical

Imagine for a moment that you were born with an enchanted Map to guide you on your journey from your first breath all the way to when it's time to drop your body and return into Spirit. On this Map are all the places you're likely to experience. You can use it to orient yourself, find your way when you're lost, chart a course to a chosen destination, or point the way home. The Map depicts battlefields, resting spots, mountains to climb, oceans to cross, quicksand to carefully emerge from, and new territories to discover. It shows possible destinations and probable events.

The Map is unlike any you've ever seen. Most maps are two-dimensional and made of paper. They lie flat and are covered in drawings representing the lay of the land. They don't change when you look at them. When you discover new territory, you have to redraw a map and add new features and previously un-known places. You can hold it in your hand, but you can't jump into it. . . . Well, you could, but you'd end up with a big hole in the paper and a bump on your head!

The Map is very different. It's a multi-dimensional map made of thoughts, feelings, beliefs, memories, and intentions. It's made of the soul's essence of creativity and imagination.

Step into the Map and it suddenly transports you into the land you've chosen to explore. Wondering where you are? *Shazam!*

You're in a landscape, discovering things about your circumstances that were impossible to see when you were completely engulfed by your emotional experiences, unable to view them with objectivity.

And there's something else to note: The enchanted Map automatically changes when you do. A fresh perspective and a shift in perception can alter it. Its history can be rewritten, and you can create new pathways and new territories as it unfurls into your future.

You are constantly moving on the Map, able to leave your confines and check out another place whenever you choose. Once you know a place, it becomes part of your experience, and therefore, part of the Map. You have some familiarity with the terrain so that when you revisit it, you don't feel quite so lost and disoriented. You quickly remember you've got that compass to help you, and allies who will appear for you.

Your internal landscape may shift when you least expect it, but if you try to stay in rhythm with your surroundings, you can develop the ability to sense when the ground beneath your feet is about to transform. Then you can instinctively move before you fall into a crevice or slip off a mountain pass and roll down a rock-filled gulley.

When you walk blindly, the Map unfolds differently than it does when you're awake and aware. So when something someone says triggers you and you can't immediately "figure it out," you can take time out, describe the landscape with metaphor and symbol, find the wisdom, and move on without reacting. Always be aware of your ability to interact with the Map. Remind yourself, "Today, I am not in the land of disaster. I don't have to remain in this state of thought, feeling, and belief. I will find the oracle, and it will show me the way out."

Your map is unique, and no one but you will ever have it, because it tells your own personal story. No two souls' Maps are the same even if the territories and landscapes are, because no one experiences events in exactly the same way. Two people can be sitting next to each other, and one will be wandering forlorn and parched in a desert while the other is relaxing happily in a beautiful oasis.

Even so, all who have visited the Valley of Loss know what it's like to be at the bottom, looking up at hills that seem far too steep to climb, wondering how to escape to higher ground. We've all stood at the base of the Immovable Mountain, facing an obstacle that seems to block our way.

Everything that you are, have been, and ever could be is illustrated on this map. You just need to know how to use it to guide you along the twists and turns of the adventure of your life's one-of-a-kind journey.

The Map becomes visible to you when you make a conscious choice to be awake, aware of something greater than yourself, and to embrace the possibility of a pattern created by Spirit that you can't always make out from where you stand. You must be willing to see the Spirit within all things, to accept that there are millions of invisible connections behind all the events in your life. They are constantly moving, set in motion by an intelligence that you will never fully understand but must trust anyway.

As you surrender to Spirit and ask for illumination, your Enchanted Map reveals itself in all its glory, and you realize that in your pocket is a compass that always points to true north: to Spirit, whose guidance will never fail you and whose efforts on your behalf never cease, whether you realize it or not.

Embrace the Magical Adventure

I believe that to find magic and meaning in your life, you first have to learn to be at peace with whatever landscape you inhabit. The more you try to escape it, the more you find yourself snapped right back to it. In fact, there may be some hidden treasure there that you can find by exploring it, finding its message by understanding its essence. In every landscape there is an oracle, and I will teach you how to communicate with oracles in this book.

Are you frustrated or unhappy with where you are at the moment? This "place" is simply one spot on the Map. You can stay here and find all the hidden treasures or listen to the stories the rocks whisper to the wind, or you can move forward into someplace new. You can see where you've been and even revisit those places, but as the saying goes, you can't step into the same river twice. And this location, or any other, is only temporary anyway, because the Map is always changing.

There are seasons and cycles for everything. No storm stays in one place, so even if you are in the turbulent seas, fearing your boat will capsize, the winds *will* move along, as they always do, and the waters will become still once more. It may be that by exploring this landscape and discovering its hidden treasures, you'll find that there is nothing you have to "do" to escape it. It alters because *you've* transformed. Experience this and you'll realize that your life doesn't have to be such a struggle.

All of us need to reconcile ourselves to the paradox that change is the only constant. Animals migrate, winds blow, the earth rotates, and the planets revolve around the sun. You, too, are moving, engaged in a journey. Through a simple adjustment to your perception, you can elevate that journey to a mystical, magical adventure.

Because this is an adventure, you're going to experience some drama along the way: danger, intrigue, romance, and celebration. Stuff happens. There will be rocky roads, steep hills, and crystal lakes. In the epic fantasy by J. R. R. Tolkien *The Lord of the Rings,* the story begins in the sweet safety of the Shire and moves into the fiery, hellish territory of Mordor. The *Harry Potter* series places the boy wizard in a dark and unfriendly English "Muggle" home and then plays out the narrative in Hogwarts School of Witchcraft and Wizardry, where staircases shift suddenly underneath him. *The Wizard of Oz* transports Dorothy Gale from her home in Kansas to the magical land of Oz, where a yellow brick road winds through Munchkinland, the enchanted forest, and the Emerald City.

Every great tale contains many different terrains, each with its own challenges, secrets, and treasures that echo our own inner landscapes. These stories are about ordinary characters who, like many of us, feel out of place and unsure that they belong wherever it is that they find themselves. Nevertheless, they venture forth and confront danger and temptation as they try to achieve what we all want: the feeling of being at home, at peace, and in a state of joy that can be shared with loyal friends and companions. The adventurers in each tale are looking for purpose, for evidence that their suffering and struggles have made a difference.

We, too, can always find people who will offer love, encouragement, and their own special gifts at crucial points in our narrative arc: a rope to rescue us from the snake pit, or a lantern that will illuminate the path when darkness falls. We, too, can find meaning, magic, and a balance between a desire to create something better for ourselves and a longing for respite. Life doesn't have to be an exhausting, nonstop chase scene. We don't have to be stuck for ages in a jungle with hostile monkeys. Even Indiana Jones returned to civilization to teach an archaeology class once in a while.

Your Inner Allies and Challengers

As you work with your Map, you'll need to confront aspects of yourself that may be painful or frightening to look at because you find them ugly or because you feel you're not entitled to embrace something so beautiful and valuable. These are the "shadow" elements described by Jung, because they hide in the shadows of your subconscious.

I've created mythological imaginary characters you can interact with in your inner landscapes so that you can acknowledge, accept, and learn from these forgotten or repressed parts of yourself. It's a lot easier to face a mythical Goblin who represents the part of you that believes you're unlikable or unworthy and interact with him, than to take on the persona of someone who is unlovable and insignificant and then try to accept that "self."

Working with shadow elements, the parts of yourself that you wish you could disown, takes courage, but I want you to imagine that you have the power to tame this sabotaging creature called the Goblin. You'll find that you can feel compassion for him despite his hideousness, love him, and uncover his value and importance in your life. The Goblin, like all the imaginary creatures and beings you meet in these pages, is simply a metaphor for some part of you that is wounded and needs nurturing, not judgment; and acceptance, not admonishment.

Every one of us has a Goblin or two who needs and deserves love. When compassion for these aspects of ourselves eludes us, Spirit is there to fill us with love and acceptance.

Over the years, I've found the Goblin character I've created incredibly effective for helping people with deep healing. (If you're new to my work, I first introduced the metaphor of the Goblin in my book *Remembering the Future*.) You have to know where you are and look your Goblin in the eye if you're to begin to take the driver's seat in your life, for he is the part of you that will send you careening from one distressing emotional landscape to another with hardly a breath in between.

You don't have to be at the mercy of this trickster who fancies himself a transportation engineer. However, you do need to stop fighting, denying, or disowning him, which only creates more trouble for you. (You'll learn a lot more about your relationship with this mischievous fellow and other archetypal characters within you later in the book.)

All of the enchanted beings you meet are symbols brought to life through your imagination, and represent aspects of your psyche. They serve as powerful metaphors for your inner wisdom and for the wisdom of Spirit, which is always available to you. The lessons you learn through inner conversations with them may surprise you, because you probably often underestimate just how wise you are once you turn off the chatter of your ever-busy mind and access your intuition and inner knowing.

Sometimes what you learn is painful; sometimes it's inspiring. But know that whether an inner imaginary being appears to be a challenger bearing bad news or an ally bearing insights, this part of yourself is always, ultimately, a helper for you if you work with him, her, or it effectively.

As you journey through common familiar territories that are at once intimate and universal, you can consult your magical compass and receive guidance from these allies and challengers on this map who know the lay of the land and all its secrets.

Whenever you're experiencing scarcity, an oracle who resides in this landscape—the Spirit of the place—will reveal to you its secret gifts. Trust in your ability to interact with this magic map and its living parts . . . and you'll recognize that you're never, ever trapped or alone.

Wherever you are, whatever emotional turbulence you're experiencing, you can learn to be present with it for just as long as you need to be, and no more. In every land, there are questions to be answered and discoveries to be made, all of which empower you as a magical mapmaker. Call up the Map and know your place in it, and you'll learn how to find the courage to be fully present in your circumstances and to trust in your burgeoning ability to navigate to higher ground. You'll learn to let your soul awaken to the power within you and use it for the good of all.

How to Use This Book

Within these pages, you'll take a journey away from fear, despair, worry, anger, or frustration and claim your power as a magical mapmaker.

— In **Part I**, you'll explore the answer to the question: "Where are you?" Your inner world is represented by a landscape you interact with and can influence. Here, you'll learn about the ever-reliable Compass of Spirit that can guide you far better than mere logic can. This compass awakens you to your ability to co-create magic in your life.

You'll come to recognize that if you stop trying to run and just take a deep breath and begin exploring this landscape, you'll start to free yourself from the feeling of being tossed about from one distressing and disorienting land to another. You'll discover how to more confidently traverse the Storm Fields, Valley of Loss, and Sticky Swamp so that you might rejuvenate under the Resting Tree or on Easy Street, or experience the marvelous views from the Peaks of Joy that can be found on the borders of all challenging landscapes.

Wherever you are, you're also somewhere in time. You can think about the past and ponder the future, and it's your task to recognize how to "time-travel" effectively so you don't feel lost on the Map of your life. In this part of the book, you'll also discover what to do if you wander off into the Ghostlands because you've indulged too long in nostalgia or wishful thinking instead of focusing on what you can do right now.

— In **Part II**, you'll begin to navigate your map. You'll learn to recognize the influence of the trickster Goblin who represents your wounded ego and distinguish his voice so that you can keep him from constantly manipulating you. You'll also learn how this crafty creature sneaks into your inner dialogues about your everyday life, dialogues represented by the Chatterbox, who is the personification of your healthy, unwounded ego. Then you'll meet inner magical allies who populate the landscapes of your enchanted Map and discover how they can help you. I'll provide you with plenty of exercises that will allow you to use your subconscious wisdom to learn more about your past, present, and future and how you can reduce your suffering and begin healing your wounds.

These dialogues involve visualization, but there is always a journal component as well. The exercises will be far more effective if you commit to working with a journal where you can record your experiences using them, including the details of your "enchanted" conversations with the magical beings. It can be extremely helpful to come back to such writings in the future to see how far you've come and what you've learned. Keep in mind that when I ask you to "write" about your experiences and impressions, you should feel free to draw them instead.

In these exercises, you'll work with the Wizard of Awareness, the observing self that sees with the neutral eyes of the soul. You'll dialogue with, and tame, the trickster Goblin, who whisks you away to harrowing landscapes where you have the opportunity to evolve, and acquire wisdom. You'll follow the Bone Collector as she beckons you to reclaim what is rightfully yours or what you've been denied, and then say hello to her twin sister, the Gentle Gardener. This kindly Mother Earth figure will show you how to plant your seeds of intention in the Field of Dreams, where she will help you grow all that you desire.

You'll also work with the Spirits of Place: Ancient myths contained tales of these living spirits in nature, and I've adapted this idea to help you discover what you need to know in any setting you find yourself in. The Spirits of Place will reveal the light and shadow in any emotional landscape, illumine the treasures in this land, and teach you how to forge a talisman of power and courage that you can carry with you always.

— In **Part III**, you'll come to a less-challenging leg of your journey and take a breather from emotionally difficult twists and turns (finally!). Here, you'll quietly reflect on the meaning and magic you've been seeking and begin to see that like every human being, you're on a hero's journey of discovery; of healing; and of striving toward greater abundance, joy, and security. You'll learn how magic reveals itself in your life and provides the sense of purpose you long for, and find out how to work with this magic.

— Last, in **Part IV**, you'll begin to look at how your map interacts with others' and apply all that you've learned so that you can begin to forge better relationships, find supportive traveling companions, and bid farewell to those whose journeys no longer align with yours. All people's maps are constantly weaving new patterns as they intersect, which is evident in fate points, synchronicities, and meetings with the ones I call Magical Map Shifters, who dramatically alter your course.

You will find allies and challengers in your life because they, too, are meant to help you become a better mapmaker. As you work with your Map to make your life a mystical, wondrous adventure, you affect the world and it affects you. New people and opportunities present themselves. Where will you go, now that you are a conscious mapmaker? You'll learn about that in the final chapter of the book.

In all the other chapters, you'll find Traveler's Notes that summarize the main points of the material you've just read. If you're like most people, you probably tend to rush through life, not truly taking in its wisdom, not stopping to process all that you've learned. If you've ever kept a travel diary, you know how much value there is in taking notes on the places you visit, the people you meet, the sights you see, and the experiences you have. If you don't keep notes, the memories begin to blur, and you can't recall all the exquisite details of your journey.

I encourage you to come back again and again to the Traveler's Notes; ponder them; and record in your journal any thoughts, impressions, or feelings they inspire, adding your own newfound wisdom to them.

Also, as you're working with concepts presented here, feel free to let your intuition generate other magical landscapes that will help you interact with your inner feelings, thoughts, and beliefs in an emotionally safe way. You'll find a List of Magical Places at the end of this book to help you remember the lands you've explored in these pages. You might also take inspiration from the familiar lands of fantasy and fairy tales. Movies and books such as *The Wizard of Oz,* the *Harry Potter* series, *Avatar,* and *The Lord of the Rings* have been extremely successful around the world because they feature wondrous landscapes where archetypal stories that resonate for people everywhere play out.

We immerse ourselves in these adventures with their hair-raising, sharp turns that are softened and straightened by the presence of magic, which allows a humble boy named Harry to fend off great evil. It illumines the path of the Avatar in a forest that appears dangerous at first but reveals itself to be nurturing once he embraces a new way of living and perceiving. The magic we enjoy in such movies and books is operating in our own daily lives, but we may not yet have observed it.

By working with the technique of traveling to enchanted inner landscapes and talking to mystical creatures, you can rediscover the magic that exists alongside mundane reality, just as the world of Hogwarts and the wizards in *Harry Potter* exists alongside that of the ordinary "Muggles." But to do so, you must quiet your logical mind. Then you can discover the hidden wonders that unfold when you sit in the chair belonging to the Wizard of Awareness and open the eyes of your soul.

A Collective Journey

You are not alone on this journey, nor are you alone if you feel "lost" on the Map of your life. Many people today are feeling that it's hard to make sense of their lives.

There's a strained, out-of-sync relationship between the reality all of us are experiencing and the one we long to inhabit. In this time of tremendous change and a stirring global awareness of our interconnectedness, too many of us are feeling powerless, fearful, confused, and anxious. Yet we're also feeling excited about the positive transformations to come. What we know for sure is that change is rapidly upon us.

There's a lot of talk these days about 2012 and what that may or may not mean. The End of Days? The Apocalypse? Many experts have studied the ancient Mayan calendar, the Hopi prophecies, and other commentaries on these times; and although conclusions and details vary, the common thread of thought is the same: we're leaving an old way of being and entering a new Great World Age. Many scholars, both ancient and modern, speak about the evolution of humanity, about endings and new beginnings. All of them point to this crucial time in our planetary history as one of tremendous transformation. But what kind of change will we experience?

Without a doubt, we're all being called to release the old ways of being in the world that no longer sustain us, and enter unknown territory. We'll do so because we recognize that it's no longer possible to find our security in the outer forms we've been conditioned to trust, whether it's economic systems or national borders. We must find a new way of orienting ourselves so that we don't feel lost, or at the whim of the fates, as institutions and systems and the circumstances of our lives begin to transform dramatically.

We change the world from the inside out, and that's why I've written this book. I wish to guide you in finding peace within regardless of what is going on in your life. You'll learn proven methods to shift your awareness so you can do what's needed to transform the outer world into a better place for yourself and for all of us.

Where are we going? Called into the unknown, we must learn to be our own oracles. An *oracle* taps into the greater, Divine wisdom that transcends our small ideas of personal survival and our limited notions about the possibilities before us. Spirit gifts us with new eyes that are open to potential. We can embrace our souls' destiny no matter what difficulties are presented in the temporary outer conditions of our lives.

At this transitional time, as we shift into a new consciousness, we all yearn for a map so we can see where we're going. It's been a long journey, and we're still on it. Each of us can choose to work with our map consciously, become magical mapmakers, and alter our course. Then we'll bring healing to this world, and at the same time find the meaning we seek.

Much as we might long for a reliable shortcut to an idyllic spot, we rarely find it. There's no detour around suffering and painful lessons, around the distressing landscapes of our lives. All of us have to visit these darker places because that is part of our adventure. However, we don't have to stay for long or keep revisiting them over and over. We have a choice—but only if we claim it for ourselves. Then we find we have the power to go home, to the place inside of us where we feel secure, safe, and loved.

And here's something curious: whenever we do get to a gentle resting place, we soon find ourselves yearning to move forward after a while, because without movement, there is no life!

Because you're human, it is your nature to journey, to discover that what you've been looking for is all around you. Very often the grassy spot you seek is right under your feet. You just need to awaken to that knowledge that's hidden from your conscious mind.

Yes, you're wearing ruby slippers and can go home anytime you like. For now, embrace this grand adventure. Step into the enchanted Map of you. . . .

Part 1

ORIENTING YOURSELF ON YOUR MAP

Author's Note: Most of the stories in this book are true accounts in which the names and identifying details have been changed to protect confidentiality, while a few stories are composites drawn from years of work with thousands of clients. The latter are true to the spirit of teaching, although not to the experience of any particular individual.

Chapter One

WHERE ARE YOU?

"You have to leave the city of your comfort and go into the wilderness of your intuition . . . what you'll discover will be wonderful. What you'll discover is yourself."

— ALAN ALDA

"Every one of us has in him a continent of undiscovered character. Blessed is he who acts the Columbus to his own soul."

— AUTHOR UNKNOWN

Once upon a time, there was a woman who had a harrowing adventure on her enchanted Map. This dramatic story took place over the course of several years as she found herself bounced from one landscape to another because she was scared, and unwilling to explore what she needed to learn in each place:

> *All around me, the air was crackling. I ran through the dark fields, seeking shelter and light, frightened by the storm. Thunder boomed and shook the earth as bolts of lightning cracked open*

3

the sky, briefly illuminating the landscape. Everything began to catch fire, and I watched the fragile paper walls of my home burn away. I had been here for so long, yet I didn't really know what this place was; I just knew I wanted "out," so I kept running.

Suddenly, I was in a field of scarlet poppies that stretched as far as the eye could see. I could hear them whispering to me: "Stay, sleep, dream . . . be ours and only ours." Relieved, and so very tired, I lay my head on the soft bed of flowers and felt myself falling into a sleepy stupor. For a brief moment, I flashed back to where I'd been before the lightning struck. It was a barren wasteland, an eerie and desolate place where none of my seeds grew and the parched ground gasped for cool rain that never came. Life had been such a struggle, so unfair. Who stole my water? Who took my dreams?

I fell into the deep slumber of denial that accompanied alcoholism and addiction. Abuse, alcohol, food, a man? Spending, alcohol, drugs, starving, bingeing, a new soul mate? Abuse? . . . on and on and on.

The thunder cracked. I was back in the Storm Fields, running desperately. In my panic, I felt my frustration rising as I remembered how often I'd been here before. I swore as I tripped over a root and stumbled on a rock, and vaguely realized that the dry earth under my feet was the very land of desolation where I had dwelled for years. Rain began to pelt me, and I was stunned by confusion and rage. <u>Why me?</u> I cursed my luck and the land that had been so unyielding, so unwilling to bear fruit for me.

No, I hadn't watered it or tended my seedlings—but still, I was angry. I didn't belong here. I deserved better! Who stole the sun? Who stole my story? The poppy field—where was the entrance? Oh yes, now I remembered. I heard the blossoms whispering again. All I needed to do was take the magic potion and I could return to my sweet narcotic slumber.

I was that hapless traveler who felt her life was out of control. That is *my* story, and it was years before I could find the meaning in my suffering or see the magic in how it all unfolded.

What about you? Have you been to these lands I described? Are you in one of them right now? Close your eyes and ask yourself, *Where am I?*

Can you name this land? You calm the winds and steady the earth beneath you when you give this place you find yourself in a name. Identify your inner landscape as the "Valley of Loss" and you start to recognize that you're *not* lost after all. This is simply one land on the Map of your life. As soon as you define your location, you access your powers of observation—and, as you'll learn, those are magical powers indeed.

Let go of your fear and face your surroundings, and you'll also call up your power to alter your experience of them and even change the landscape itself. You instantly awaken that part of your psyche that knows that your experiences aren't the sum of who you are. Having created a mental separation from the you who is walking through the Valley of Loss or climbing up the path of the Immovable Mountain, you recognize that you're only here temporarily, regardless of what happens. "You" exist outside of the drama and the suffering. The "you" who says, "Ah, this is where I am," and points to the Map, is your *soul.*

The "you" who is the Mapmaker and the adventurer holds the power to take you someplace better, but you no longer feel the need to do so quickly while in a blind panic. You can begin to explore this enchanted land to see what you can discover.

Your inner landscape reflects your feelings and the thoughts that are connected to them. The ground beneath you and the atmosphere around you can shift in an instant as you react to what you perceive is happening in your life. Thrust into a new landscape by a powerful emotional reaction to your circumstances, unsure of where you are, you find that your eyes are blinded by fear, self-loathing, or sorrow; and you have one simple and frantic thought: *Get me out of here!*

But what if you choose not to leave? What hidden treasures might you find? Could you at last discover your purpose, and finally understand the meaning behind the suffering you've experienced? What if you knew that you had the power to take yourself to any land you wished to visit, and that you're never a prisoner in any emotional experience?

Of course, when your heart begins to pound and your breathing becomes shallow, it's only natural to feel angry, betrayed, or victimized and to desperately reach for an anchor of calm or scramble for safety on a rock as you're tossed about by ocean swells. To stay here may seem unimaginable in the moment when your emotions are strong and painful. Even so, whenever you feel threatened—or engulfed by anger, sadness, or a sense that you're not good enough—you can step back and view this scene from the safety of your mind (with its vast potential for imagination) and retrieve your Compass of Spirit. Such moments are the points at which magic can happen.

The Places You've Been

Where have you been in your life? What emotional lands have you traversed? Did you grow up in a peaceful meadow, where the weather was gentle and predictable, or on a raging sea where you clung to a fragment of a metaphorical broken boat? Was your first day of school like visiting an adventure park or like getting caught in a maze at twilight?

If you track your experiences, you'll see all the different places you've visited on your adventure. Maybe you hit Rock Bottom and found a treasure trove full of diamonds in the dirt. Maybe you've spent most of your life in Shouldville, pleasing others at your own expense. Perhaps you've spent years wandering in a dry, Barren Desert until one day you surrendered and found a way to a real oasis.

There are many places on your Map—some very familiar, some visited only rarely . . . some delightful and some distressing. In the following exercise, you'll learn how to identify these places and recognize their features. You'll see how these landscapes operate, and distinguish how you move from one to another.

Exercise: Where Have You Been?

In this exercise, you'll take a mini-tour of your life, focusing on a chapter that had a particularly strong emotional charge at the time but which you now have some emotional distance from: a major relationship breakup or loss, a time of great upheaval, a rocky beginning to a new adventure, or some other trial that you moved through. Choose a past experience that was upsetting back then but eventually gave way to a more positive time of life.

In your journal, write a short factual narrative of what you went through. Explain what happened, what thoughts and feelings you experienced, and what actions you took. Be sure to include your beliefs at the time.

When you're finished, rewrite the story, breaking it up into a list of the events and your emotional responses to them.

Next, as you look at the list, imagine each separate experience as a landscape. Feeling betrayed when your lover left would be one landscape, while feeling grief afterward and not wanting to date again would be another.

Here's an example, with the original events of the story in boldface, followed by the landscapes my client identified. Notice that she described how she interacted with each one, as well as its features and how they changed.

Maggie was a very successful stockbroker who lost her job and was out of work for over a year. She had a few offers, but nothing panned out. Looking back, she came up with the following:

I was very worried about my prospects and feeling scared that I didn't know where or when I'd find another job. *I was wandering in a dry desert with nowhere to hide, without water or shelter, unsure of where to go to find what I needed.*

Every morning I woke up feeling anxious. I dreaded facing the day. *As soon as I opened my eyes, I felt like I was on a raft, about to go over a giant angry waterfall, but somehow my raft got suspended just before plunging downward. I was surrounded by water, but it wasn't water I could drink. Then as soon as my day got going, I'd be back in the desert, trudging along and feeling scared that I wouldn't reach my destination.*

I got job leads that didn't pan out. *These were like mirages that offered an illusion of safety.*

I met Dave, who made a good salary, and we started dating. I talked myself into believing the relationship had real potential when I knew deep down it didn't— that it was a distraction seducing me with the prospect of financial security. *I felt I had found an oasis, but every time I reached out to drink from the spring, it began to fade. Before it could vanish, I'd step back and convince myself I could make it a little longer—that the water there was real—but when I'd try to take a drink again later, it was always a mirage. Scared, I clung to the illusion of the misty oasis.*

Finally, I felt I was going to have a breakdown if I didn't get some certainty in my life—a job, or a sign that my relationship was solid. So I started going to a yoga class; joined a prayer group; went for many walks; took time to read good books; began to feel humble; and did odd jobs for friends, helping out however I could. I wondered if I really wanted the job I was looking for. *I felt the sand beneath my feet shifting and noticed raindrops landing on my face. A steady, nurturing rain began to fall; and I saw that the desert was sprouting life. I began to trust; then I surrendered to the fact that this desert journey showed me how to be patient, resilient, and resourceful.*

I began sleeping better, feeling less stressed-out and more hopeful. When Dave said he didn't want to continue the relationship, a sense of relief came over me, and I ended up wishing him well. *The weather changed. It wasn't so hot or dry; things were just nice and temperate.*

Finally, I was offered another job. *I can only describe it as coming around a bend on a winding mountain path and suddenly discovering a meadow with a huge patch of brilliant wildflowers. I felt that I was on a friendly mountain and that it* *was speaking to me, saying, "You see? I have many wonderful surprises. Keep climbing!" I got to the top and knew I could do something else. The vista was incredible!*

I changed professions after I reached the top of the mountain. I left finance, moved to the country, and opened a pie shop! I am in Adventure Land, having a fun time, and excited about what each new day holds.

As you look at what *you* have written, do you see how the landscape changed at times because of choices you made and at times because of circumstances that felt out of your control—events, emotional responses in the moment, ideas that suddenly came to you, or opportunities that opened up? Do you see how you interacted with your Map? You're *always* interacting with it, but now you can do so consciously.

Where are you today? What emotional landscape are you inhabiting? Is it where you'd like to be? Do you feel you belong here?

The Reliable Compass of Spirit

Whenever we feel lost or out of place, we can turn to Spirit to guide us and orient us on our map.

Spirit is a force like the magnetic pull of the north pole. Spirit is true north, the Source of all power and wisdom, and it will never mislead you. The Divine is always present, even when you lose track of where it is. You're a spiritual being learning through a human form, and therefore you're already magnetic to Spirit. Somewhere inside you, you have a natural pull to Spirit that will always guide you correctly. All you need to do is slow down and pull out your compass. As you remain still, Spirit speaks to you through intuition, orienting you, then pointing you to the next right action or soul lesson. It's your personal GPS!

Consult it . . . and then, as you breathe a sigh of relief, you'll recognize that you're not alone and lost in the woods. You'll see that you're on the enchanted Map and have the power to influence your experience—to rescue yourself from being mired in the Sticky Swamp, or feeling guilty and overwhelmed in Shouldville.

You'll also discover that the act of taking out your compass has caused you to summon the enchanted creatures who will serve as your mentors, allies, and challengers. These personified aspects of your psyche will always tell you what you need to know, which may be very different from what you want to hear!

If you don't listen to their wisdom, however, and you ignore their presence, you'll forget all about your compass and misplace it. You'll find yourself racking your brain to figure out what went wrong and how to avoid suffering and get what you want out of life. Then your adventure will feel more like a nightmare, and you'll start to believe you're powerless when, in fact, you have enormous potential for directing your course.

Here's an example: Imagine that your mother-in-law calls you up at the beginning of your day and lays a guilt trip on you. She's always so negative, and normally you can handle it, but your husband has just lost his job and you might have to find one, your house might have to be sold, and your two kids are at college and constantly calling to ask for more money. You're a spiritual person, right? You know all the metaphysical answers and affirmations, but you can't remember anything at that moment, and your reaction throws you over a metaphorical cliff.

Take out your compass and align with true north, with Spirit, and you'll see where you are. Maybe you feel you're in Shouldville, or in that harrowing landscape known as the Storm Fields. Maybe it's as if you're in the mud somewhere in the jungle, the air humid and sticky, and you're being pelted with poop thrown at you by a whole lot of monkeys hiding in the trees who scream at you as you try to duck the oncoming manure. Awful as this "place" may seem, you're not stuck here. Those monkeys are *yours,* and you can get them to stop annoying you . . . and when you do so, you'll find that the landscape magically shifts into a more peaceful one.

How do you go about this? By using the magical cartographer's techniques described in this book, all of which can help you move out of being reactive and become more creative. You change your inner landscape and, as a result, your outer one as well. You look around this familiar monkey-infested jungle and remember what to do to escape: you consciously decide not to give weight to your mother-in-law's words, and you simply tell her, "I hear what you're saying—thank you for sharing," end the call, and turn your mind back to what it was you really wanted to focus on.

As you'll learn, such transformations out of emotional drama and into calm waters truly are possible. All the power to change that instant reaction of anger, frustration, and helplessness is at hand if you pull out your Compass of Spirit.

The Faulty Compass of Logic

What about logic? How does the analytical mind fit into this? After all, facts are facts, and there are reasonable things to do when the world is falling apart and people are pushing your buttons! Logic has its benefits, but when you use it as your *only* guidance tool, instead of letting Spirit direct you, your thinking is mechanical, and you have a mechanistic view of life that prevents you from perceiving magic and mystery. You limit your enchanted powers.

A logical mind tries to make sense of it all, which is a noble aim, but one that none of us can achieve! We don't have the capacity to understand everything that happens in life or to figure out how to change our circumstances and alter the behavior of other people. None of us can know why an earthquake or tidal wave occurs and thousands of people die as a result, or what we personally can do to "fix" these overwhelming problems of the human condition. We could drive ourselves mad trying to ascertain what we might have done to "attract" the pickpocket who stole our wallet, the chronic ailment with no known cause, or the relative who can't seem to respect our boundaries.

Some things just happen. Using logic all on its own to dissect the disparate events of life can sometimes tell you how things have happened and may also provide information that might help you in preventing future disasters. But logic can't show you the underlying causal forces, can't reveal the mystery or the magic, and can't answer the question *Why?*

The Compass of Spirit reminds you that you can trust that your heart will most likely continue to beat, air will continue to fill your lungs, and, if you make good choices and work hard, your life won't be as difficult as it would be if you made poor choices and left all the struggle for someone else. As much as you'd like to believe that you can avoid irritation, frustration, pain, and tragedy altogether, it's just not going to happen—and that drives the logical mind crazy.

You can't "figure out" how to fix your life so that nothing bad and unexpected will happen to you. You can, however, choose to embrace a mystical journey; work with the symbols that serve as the language of mystery and Spirit; and live a richer, deeper life that can't be planned to the last detail.

If you surrender to the adventure and trust in your Compass of Spirit, then the Map will begin to make sense, and new paths will reveal themselves.

Spirit is the antidote for every type of suffering we create for ourselves. Working with an imaginary Compass of Spirit that reminds us of the loving, comforting power of the Divine can help us remember that whenever we are lost, it's only an illusion, because Spirit is right there with us.

The following exercise will help *you* feel the power and presence of the Divine.

Exercise: Orient Yourself on the Magic Compass

As with a real compass, you'll be working with four directions: *N, S, E,* and *W.* However, instead of these letters representing "north," "south," "east," and "west," they stand for emotional experiences and perceptions (as you'll see).

Draw a compass face on a piece of paper (whether real or in your mind): Label the needle pointing upward "N," the downward-facing needle "S," the one pointing to the right "E," and the one pointing to the left "W." Underneath the *N*, write: "True North." Then under *E*, write: "Ego"; under *W*, write: "Willfulness"; and under *S*, write: "Separation."

Place the compass on the floor, with *N* oriented upward, just as on a map. Stand up, close your eyes, and breathe in and out slowly. Feel your connection to Spirit. True north never alters, never moves. It is always there for you.

Now turn 90 degrees to the right, to the direction of "Ego." Meditate on what *ego* means to you. What images, thoughts, feelings, or sensations come to you when you think of this word? Do you experience a flash of memory of a time when you were ruled by your ego, a moment when you let it be in charge? Do you think of occasions when you felt unheard or unappreciated? Do you *feel* unappreciated? Invisible? Do you feel shame, or a sense that you're undeserving in some way? Whatever your thoughts, beliefs, or memories, however unsettling or painful they may be, remain present with them. Allow yourself to express your emotions with your body. Take as long as you need in order to understand what the experience of "ego" is.

When you're ready, turn another 90 degrees to the right so that you're facing *S,* or "Separation." Take a few moments to focus on the word *separation* and notice what images, thoughts, feelings, or sensations come to you. How does it feel to experience "separation"? What memories arise? Do you feel lonely? Do you see yourself trying too hard to please others in an attempt to convince them to let you into their group? Are you remembering junior high school and its cliques?

When you're ready, turn your body again so that you're facing "Willfulness," or *W*. Meditate on *willfulness*. What does it mean to you? How does it make you feel? What images come to mind when you experience a connection to willfulness? When you're willful, do others respond as you'd like them to? Do your circumstances conform to your expectations? Does willfulness "work" for you or leave you frustrated?

Return to the position of "True North." Feel yourself reconnecting with the power of Spirit's unconditional love for you.

Imagine a white light surrounding you and infusing you with protective, nurturing love. You feel safe, liberated, and courageous. Savor this experience for a few minutes.

No matter where you turn, Spirit is there, as you will experience next.

Retrieve your compass and cross out "Ego," "Separation," and "Willfulness" and replace them with "Effortlessness," "Surrender to the Sacred," and "We." Repeat this exercise, facing each direction and meditating on these empowering, loving experiences. Finish by experiencing true north again. Then, take out a journal and write about the images, thoughts, beliefs, feelings, and memories that came to you.

The points on this Compass of Spirit alter when you recognize the transformative power of the Divine.

You no longer need to perceive your separateness and can instead feel and enjoy being part of *we,* a larger community of people and of creatures on planet Earth.

You can bypass your ego's need to feel important, recognized, and heard through *surrender to the Sacred.* You'll find security in knowing that Spirit is always watching out for you, always working on your behalf. You can trust its loving guidance and defer to its wisdom.

You can replace your willfulness with *effortlessness* as you patiently await the miracles of Spirit, parting the sea that stands as an obstacle before you, giving you wings to transcend your troubles, offering you possibilities you would never have thought of, and bringing into your life people and situations that reflect your inner calm and acceptance.

At any time, you can pull out the compass that aligns you with the invisible force of true north; orient yourself in a place that has you confused, sad, scared, or frustrated; and become an observer of this experience. Then the real magic of your life begins, and you remember why you came here.

Whenever you come to those places where your emotions rise and begin to form funnel clouds that threaten to engulf you, know that you're standing at an intersection between two worlds, where the invisible forms and informs the visible. If you can step back from yourself and accept that you are here, where X marks the spot, you'll remember that *you* are not your inner landscape. You are not the Storm Fields that churn inside of you, the Barren Desert that has you feeling forlorn and living in scarcity. You are not the Raging River that sends you hurtling downstream with the current.

As you travel through different landscapes, you're always able to see yourself as a separate participant. You're not a grieving person, but someone temporarily traveling through the Valley of Loss, a zone you can choose to walk out of (although you may have to return at some point). You're a brave explorer and powerful being who just realized you're not where you want to be, and you have the power to take yourself someplace else.

Confusion about Our "Place"

In a recent seminar, I asked 150 participants, "How many of you are lost right now?" and all but a handful raised their hands.

It's happening to all of us. We may know where our chairs are, but we're lost in another environment altogether. If that's true, then *where are we?*

Human beings are the only species that doesn't have a true sense of "place." This is because we're able to use our minds to imagine ourselves somewhere else, to revisit the past and imagine the future. We experience a reality other than the present moment, a reality called our subjective experience, which is often at odds with the events going on outside of our heads. No wonder we're disoriented. Our emotions and our thoughts have us in a desert when we're sitting in a seminar in a hotel room.

All of us have a "place" within the world, and within the great web of life. Knowing this "place" gives us a sense of security and purpose. The problem is that we give so much weight to our own internal experiences that we have amnesia about our true nature, and then we can't find our home, where we belong. We feel as if we're wandering aimlessly on winding roads to who knows where. We forget that we're adventurers on an Enchanted Map, engaged in the magical art of co-creation with our fellow travelers and Spirit. We can't go "home" until we know where we are right now.

I felt lost and confused, tossed around from the Barren Desert to the Storm Fields to the hypnotic Field of Poppies for years, until I finally hit Rock Bottom and recognized that I was an alcoholic who was powerless over my drinking. I had fallen asleep in that dangerously alluring Field of Poppies so often that I'd missed out on much of life and many chances to grow, to heal myself, and to embrace my purpose. I had simply been existing as I reacted to what was happening all around me. I hadn't been able to hear the voice of my soul, which knew where home was and how to get there.

I couldn't own my role in co-creating the events of my life, because that thought was far too painful to entertain. Deeply uncomfortable in my inner landscape, I was frantically seeking a place of respite that kept eluding me. And like many alcoholics, I had a *Shazam!* moment when I one day peered into a mirror with a very different pair of eyes. I truly saw myself for the first time in as long as I could remember.

The Mirror Never Lies

People will often say that it's a photograph of themselves, a video clip, or a reflection in a mirror that jolts them out of their sleepwalking and alerts them to who they are and what they're doing. *Shazam!* They see themselves as they are right now, not as they wish themselves to be or remember themselves being. They're able to do this because they've stepped out of their subjective emotional experience and become aware of their observing self, who sees with great clarity. The wizard who can change the Map is awake! The soul speaks!

Neuroscience shows that when your nervous system is experiencing a panic response to perceived danger, the blood flow and electrical activity in the part of your brain that allows you to run away or put up a fight increases. At the same time, the part of the brain that allows you to contemplate, control your impulses, plan, and dream becomes inactive; and consequently, you can't think straight.

This is why it seems that you become "blinded" by jealousy and rage, or "overcome" with grief. Your calm, observing self is asleep, because these powerful emotions are blocking you from accessing the potential of your brain to rise above the pain of the moment. But if you can awaken that ability, you can survey the landscape of your thoughts, feelings, and beliefs. You can look at yourself and recognize there are two selves: the "you" who is experiencing this landscape, and the "you" who is watching this happen.

Although the awakening of your observing self—the consciousness that isn't feeling confused, lost, or overwhelmed—may happen in a *Shazam!* moment, you might have already developed the ability to step outside yourself. Everyone has the power within to embrace that skill of rousing the observing self that can reflect. Have you forgotten that *you* have this ability? Do you sometimes catch yourself observing that you're not your emotional experience, saying, *Hmm, I'm really flipping out here. Could I be overreacting?*

We're not always in the habit of listening to that inner voice. Our attention is drawn to the drama of our landscape, and we forget that we're the ones creating it.

Have you ever had a dream where you felt you were being chased or were in grave danger, and suddenly a part of your psyche realized you were asleep and woke you up?

Our minds are set up to be self-protective, but sometimes we have to feel some pain in order to heal. We have to look into the dark places. There's no getting "around" the shadowlands, no detour.

But imagine that you have the power to awaken at any time, to reclaim your powers of observation and take up your magic wand that taps into all your inner wisdom, as well as the wealth of wisdom the Divine makes available to all of us. Imagine that your courage to face all challenges is there for you at hand, and you can instantly call upon all the enchanted creatures of this land to assist you in magically traveling to a better place.

You *can* do this. And you *will* have help.

Perception and Filters

Wherever you are, you are "here." You are where you perceive yourself to be.

Your thoughts, feelings, and beliefs create the landscape in your psyche. This is the place you truly inhabit, which can be unrelated to the place you physically inhabit.

This place is created by your perception. You see what you expect to see even if you aren't fully aware that you do expect it. The mind is wired very efficiently to look for evidence that you can apply what you've learned or experienced in the past to what you're seeing before your eyes in the moment. It's used to spotting the signs of danger and potential for suffering. That's why it's so difficult to break the patterns of thoughts and behavior that may have served a protective purpose at some point in your life but which aren't working very well for you now. Your mind, like everyone else's, is always filtering out facts that contradict what you believe.

All of us have to evolve out of this limited way of looking at our lives. We need to become mindful of our filters and learn how to change them. In this way, we empower ourselves to make different choices and create new patterns, a new story that will be illustrated on the Map.

Here's how perception works: Your brain imposes meaning and order on everything you see to make it intelligible and to simplify all the confusing and contradictory information you confront. Your conscious mind blocks out much of the sensory input that comes into the brain, and for a good reason: If you took it all in, you would go wack-a-doodle mad. It's not possible to experience all that surrounds you without becoming completely disoriented.

Scientists agree that the human mind is only able to take in approximately 5 percent of what we are exposed to, and this fraction is selected through our subconscious and organized in the prefrontal cortex of the brain.

In the age of information, the mind's habit of oversimplifying can keep you from becoming overwhelmed. Filters are good, but to sit back and let them do all the work of deciding what is important information and what can be pushed aside is to immerse yourself in the Field of Poppies. In this sleepy land, there is no evolution and no healing. You need to wake up and experience mindfulness and open-mindedness in order to grow. Like a flower, you have to open to the rain and the sunlight. You have to change the filters in your mind and let in new information, new awareness.

When I do readings for clients, invariably I will see the process by which they make their choices. Patterns repeat and become reinforced. People tend to sleepwalk from situation to situation, in denial of the true source of their suffering: their dysfunctional beliefs that are creating internal chaos and affecting their outer reality.

You can claim your magical power to see the way you choose to see: *through the eyes of compassion for yourself and for others.* What you'll discover about yourself is, at times, hideous, so you absolutely must be gentle, loving, and forgiving toward yourself. Fortunately, Spirit is always there with infinite love for you, reminding you that you're to love yourself just as you're loved by the Divine: unconditionally.

The only way to see yourself clearly is to step back from your experience and notice what you're doing to yourself. It's not anything or anyone but your mind that is transporting you to the Storm Fields or the Sticky Swamp where you feel overwhelmed. Your adventure is always taking place *behind* the lens you're looking through. Step back and trust that Spirit is there to fill you with compassion for yourself, to give you courage to see what you need to see.

Awakening Your Awareness

Although we sometimes avoid observing ourselves because we fear that what we see will be too painful, often we're not looking at ourselves and our patterns simply because we're on autopilot. We're reacting to the events in our lives and the emotions and thoughts we're having without imagining how we might create something different from our current experience.

The only way to turn off the "autopilot" setting in your mind that causes you to have instant emotional reactions of fear, doubt, anger, or anxiety is to develop the habit of awakening the observing self. This inner witness is the most powerful manifestation of your higher self, or soul. It is like a great Wizard of Awareness with a magic wand that allows him access to all knowledge.

This inner Wizard of Awareness is the part of you that recognizes that logic and reason aren't always the most effective tools to escape a distressing emotional terrain and return to a land of joy. The wizard in you can quiet your thoughts and help you transcend the murkiness caused by strong emotion. It's as if he touches his magic wand to the river of all consciousness and reconnects you to the wisdom of the universe itself. A whole new language is available to you. Spirit can speak to you through the symbols of nature and invites you to create something new: new thoughts, beliefs, and behaviors . . . new ideas and perceptions.

When *you* change, the way you see your world changes, and in a magical way, all that surrounds you begins to shift. The Enchanted Map is altered. People view you differently. You don't look the same, walk the same, or move through the world in the way you used to. Because you're interconnected with all life, the light and awareness you experience spills over onto those around you, influencing them.

So wake up that sleepy wizard. Once you do, you'll start to see the land more clearly, and you'll know where you are.

Places You Might Visit

There are numerous lands on the Map. Listed in this section are some you may encounter; a longer list is at the end of this book. There may also be territories not included here that you discover as you begin to interact with your map. When you visit these lands, note their features and find their wisdom with the help of the Spirits of Place. As you become more confident in your ability to co-create the Map, working with Spirit and interacting with your magical allies and the traveling companions you meet along the way, you may find that you're willing to visit some of the more challenging landscapes in order to fully experience your feelings and learn your lessons.

Each land has a dark side and a light side. Get to know them and work with them. No one ever wants to change when things are going well, but if you linger too long in the happier lands, you may find yourself sleeping in the Field of Poppies or wandering without substance in a Ghostland, so you must keep the journey moving forward.

I encourage you to develop a list of lands that are unique to you. What have you experienced? What adventures might you encounter on the road ahead? Can you think of landscapes you'd like to visit? Could you imagine places to replenish you? Places to find sanctuary in, build courage, or take risks? Can you envision a landscape that sends your prayers and intentions out into the world?

Your feelings, thoughts, and beliefs are the roots of your Home Tree. By entering into the Map, observing the environments created by these ever-shifting impressions, you find, truly, that you're *not* your feelings but rather the one who *feels* them. By learning this technique of working with the landscapes on an enchanted Map, you give yourself an authentic empowering gift: to be a true magical adventurer on the journey of your destiny.

In Gregg Braden's inspiring book *Secrets of the Lost Mode of Prayer,* he writes:

Feeling Is the Prayer: Ancient traditions remind us that the world around us is nothing more and nothing less than the mirror of what we've become in our lives: what we feel about our relationships with ourselves, one another, and, ultimately, God. Scientific evidence now suggests precisely the same thing; what we feel inside our bodies is carried into the world beyond our bodies.

Remember that all these places are within you to access. Immerse yourself in the journey of discovery, and never forget that you have Spirit guiding you. You will never be lost again, and you can always find your way home.

The Sticky Swamp

The swamp is like the "primordial ooze" where substances mixed and unexpected new life and conditions formed. You might end up in the Sticky Swamp when life throws you a curveball and you're caretaking for elders and young children at the same time. Or perhaps you're having to do the work of an employee who left the company (and *you* in the lurch), or are struggling with a health crisis. You might find yourself here when you haven't prioritized the things you need to do or you've procrastinated and are faced with a pile of work you can't even bear to begin.

The muck here is so thick and gooey that it may seem that you're a prisoner in the Sticky Swamp. But if you stop struggling and see it as the creative soup of potentiality and ideas that can shift your consciousness, you may be surprised by the abundance of opportunities that float to the surface. The feeling that you have too many things to do and not enough time, and that you're failing so miserably at managing your life that you're drowning, will dissipate once you learn the lesson of the Sticky Swamp: that you have to relax and stop trying to be everything to everyone.

After you've been still for some time, the Spirit of the swamp will guide you to the next right action. Soon, all will be well. Time will even stretch for you, and you'll find enough hours in the day for everything. There is an ancient saying taken from Norse runes: "We do without doing and everything gets done."

The Valley of Loss

There's a place that none of us wants to journey through: one of pain, tears, rage, sadness, and resignation. But here in the Valley of Loss we can be broken open to find a greater sense of belonging to the soul of the world. Modern Western culture doesn't have a true sense of the importance of this place, the strength we achieve and depths we plumb when we're in this valley.

Because it is such a painful place, you have to give yourself permission to remain here. It was too hard for me to allow myself healing when I lost my parents, but I wandered and explored the Valley of Loss when each one of my dogs died. I gave myself the gift of staying there awhile and faced the harder parts of my life. It was incredibly difficult to lose these furry companions who had loved me unconditionally and taught me how to be unselfish, responsible, and compassionate. Yet experiencing their loss and the gift of my broken heart opened me wide enough to complete the long and winding journey back through my parents' passing. What had been too painful a journey became doable once I'd forged the pathway to lead me back into my healing.

I was finally freed when I consciously returned to this Valley of Loss to truly accept the human frailties among my family, seeing my part in the conflict and finally forgiving us all (although it took a while). The Valley of Loss then allowed me to heal from the tragedies that had splintered us.

Someday, this place will call to you, too. If you try to avoid it or leave it too quickly, something will *truly* be lost, for the Valley of Loss is where you learn humility, gratitude, appreciation, and deeper access to your heart.

The Barren Desert

In the Barren Desert, you're exhausted and feel that your supply of creativity has dried up. Perhaps you've even given away all your water and surrounded yourself with empty wells that you feel you have to fill. It seems that nothing grows here on the parched earth. When you're called into the Barren Desert, it seems nothing good will ever grow or flourish in your life again. This place seems endless, even though you'll eventually leave it.

The Spirit of the Barren Desert will teach you to conserve what you have rather than squander it mindlessly, find nourishment in the hidden places, and dig deep to get to water. Here you discover your resourcefulness and resilience in hard times. You also learn to look for your inspiration in your latent desires, hobbies, and creative activities. When your compass points to Spirit, inspiration comes, but sometimes you're just meant to do quiet things until the *Shazam!* moment that opens up a new path. All of a sudden, you begin to see greenery appear on what was once barren, dry soil.

Codependent Land

You end up in Codependent Land when you get involved with an addict or alcoholic, or you simply become so enmeshed in other people's lives that you lose your sense of independence and self-worth. Here, you find you have a crown on your head and a false sense of power because you believe that you're somehow responsible for others' behavior. Yet *you* don't see it this way, as you may believe you're only trying to help, or love them into wellness.

You don't recognize that you're motivated by your need to feel important by fixing others. Looking into the fun-house mirrors that are all over Codependent Land, you feel that if you could contort yourself "just so," everything would be okay and the other person would be healthy, happy, and responsible . . . but this is an illusion. The more you try to manage others, the more you fall into the trapdoors on the ground or get lost in mazes constructed of thorny thickets strewn with sticky webs that wrap around you like tentacles.

In Codependent Land, the Spirit of Place asks you to reflect on healthy boundaries, abide by a rule of loving and compassionate detachment, and learn to manage your anxiety. The only way out of this place is to practice radical acceptance and live and let live. Just as Dorothy had a mantra to get out of Oz—"There's no place like home"—you have one that will help you escape from Codependent Land: "I didn't cause it, I can't cure it, and I can't control it."

There are many other landscapes you may find yourself in, some quite lovely and others very distressing. Remember, your first job upon arriving in a disturbing one is to breathe, become calm, and look around at where you are.

The next step is to ask yourself whether you've been here before, and if you have, when? When are you in time? Are you reliving the past? Is there a purpose to doing that? Why were you meant to come back here? Only by exploring the landscape can you find the answer.

Traveler's Notes

- Your thoughts, feelings, and beliefs form an internal landscape.

- Your conditioning causes your mind to filter information and seek coherence between your internal world and your external one.

- It is important to shift your beliefs and reinforce new patterns in order to perceive the world differently.

- You can learn about your internal landscapes by describing them as enchanted environments where your emotions take on attributes of the weather or the topographical aspects of the natural world—for example, the Sticky Swamp, the Valley of Loss, Rock Bottom, and so on.

- Every landscape can serve as an oracle, allowing you to access the hidden wisdom that comes from the Divine and that will empower you.

- You must be willing to remain in your inner landscape, no matter how challenging the terrain, if you're to learn the lesson of the place.

- You can always leave a landscape if it's not serving you to be there, once you understand the lesson.

- You can always consciously return by choice in order to learn something new.

~ *Chapter Two* ~

WHEN ARE YOU?

"The past is a guidepost, not a hitching post."
— ATTRIBUTED TO L. THOMAS HOLDCROFT

"The distinction between the past, present and future is only a stubbornly persistent illusion."
— ALBERT EINSTEIN

Now that you know where you are, the question is: *When are you?*

Does the emotional landscape you find yourself in right now feel familiar?

Have you been here before? When?

Being "some-when" else other than the present moment makes it difficult for you to move forward until you make peace within the interior environment you actually inhabit: the one in your mind.

The mind needs to wander the past and future at times. As humans, we're able to do so with the richness of memory and imagination, which offer us the capacity to see our lives from different perspectives, to escape the limited view of the moment. The goal is not to remain in the present always or avoid it altogether, but to be where we need to be in time at any given juncture so that we don't feel lost.

The challenge is that our culture pushes us to multitask, and we end up losing track of "when" we are in time: we mindlessly tend to our errands and responsibilities while our minds drift to past troubles, potential problems, nostalgic landscapes, and happy or fearful visions of what may come.

How often have you rehearsed the future like an actor, or sat in a meeting obsessing about a conversation you had with your lover the day before? There's a time for each of these experiences, but it's not when you're in the middle of doing something else that requires your full attention—like, say, driving your car, or talking with someone you care about who wants to discuss an important issue. You don't want to keep finding yourself "out of time," lost, and seemingly powerless to get to the place you need to be.

In this chapter, you'll learn how to use mindfulness to time-travel. First, let me remind you what to do when you've popped back into an unpleasant spot on your Map and are tempted to hide in the past (or future) rather than dealing with the emotions you're currently experiencing: you take a deep breath, pull out your compass, describe the landscape, and ask, "Is this true for me now, or am I shadowboxing with the past?" It may be that you've been temporarily called back in time, but nevertheless, the landscape will seem quite real to you until you find a way to shift over into the present.

"Oh No, Not This Place Again!"

How many times have you found yourself in a repetitive cycle you just can't seem to break? Are you back to that same old situation again, the one that makes you feel powerless and miserable? It's easy to judge yourself harshly as you think, *What happened? I* *did all that healing work and focused my intent to change my life, and now I'm back here <u>again?</u>*

There's no shame in having slipped back into old territory. We all do so when we experience our triggers, or on anniversaries of losses or events that caused us pain. Remember, we're all on an adventure that has its dramatic elements.

You can't avoid repetitive landscapes altogether, because predicaments and challenges are part of the human experience. Every Map has permanent features you can't transform, places you must visit—perhaps more than once. It would be great if you never had to return to the Valley of Loss after being there and learning its lessons, but that's not how life works. If you run away from the present moment because it's too painful, your map will correct your course as if you were on autopilot. There's a little mischievous creature called the Goblin who will trick you into visiting and revisiting these troublesome landscapes.

There is no escape from any terrain on the Map except through surrender to the present moment and accepting that you are in it, however unsettling and upsetting it may be. Denial will take you to the Field of Poppies, where you'll repeat the same experience over and over until you change it. Be here, now, and watch the magic begin as Spirit shows you the shadow and light of this land, providing you wisdom and insights that will empower you on your adventure.

Of course, when your emotional experience is so intense that it feels as if it's never going to change, it's hard to surrender to the now. As soon as you access your mind's ability to step back from the Sticky Swamp or Valley of Loss and remember that you hold the power to interact with your Map, you'll know that no feeling lasts forever and that *you* are not your emotions. Even someone you might think of as an angry person isn't angry every minute of every day. It's not that emotions sustain themselves indefinitely, but rather that you continually regenerate them.

You can't erase distressing landscapes from your map, but mindfulness will help you stay grounded in the present, where you must embrace your emotional experience.

For many of us, mindfulness—that is, the ability to keep our thoughts on the present moment—must be learned, because it's not our habit. When I first began to practice mindfulness meditation, I found it very difficult. *My* mind loves to run here and there with great enthusiasm, but I was determined to learn how to calm my thoughts. Frankly, it was excruciating in the beginning, as "now" seemed like the last place my mind wanted to visit.

I noticed that I was best at wandering around environments that had to do with unresolved past relationships and anticipating my future career successes or potential failures. Being able to accept this time-wandering habit of mine without judgment was liberating and allowed me to start developing mindfulness. I had to keep working at it; and eventually, with regular practice, I did become more mindful—and it made all the difference in the world. I believe it is essential that all of us adopt this manner of remaining present in the now, given the hysteria accompanying the collective shift we're all experiencing in these times of global upheaval.

The paradox is that just being able to recognize that your mind is "somewhere else" empowers you to *choose* where to be. To feel compassion for yourself for not being "here" right now actually brings you back into the present. And as you learn to work with your map, you'll increase your power to remain there; to leave a difficult landscape when you're meant to, not prematurely; and to avoid unnecessary trips to lands of sorrow and suffering. You can stop feeling lost in the past or the future, running away from what you have to face.

Synchronicities and Time

When you identify the emotional landscape you're inhabiting and realize that it's overly familiar territory, it's a sign that you still haven't truly taken in the lesson of this place. You might think you have, but maybe there's wisdom here that you overlooked.

Why do you keep getting snapped back into the traumatic emotional landscapes of your past? It's because much of your interaction with the Map is *unconscious.* You have to become aware of where you are; when you are; and, as you'll see, who is guiding you. The more mindful you are, the more you'll recognize the synchronicities in your life. Then it will be much easier to remember that you have the power to get out of the repetitive landscapes where you experience suffering.

These synchronicities are actually part of Spirit's cleverly designed alarm system that alerts you to the nature of time itself so that you remember how to work with it properly and be an efficient time traveler. The idea is to be in the present most—but not all—of the time. You need to occasionally dream, reminisce, learn from the past, and prepare for a future that always involves the unexpected.

To remain in the present, you have to learn to envision the future without obsessing about the details of what will happen or trying to micromanage it. (In fact, I don't do predictive readings for people more than twice a year, because I know that it's easy to become obsessed with what *may be* instead of focusing on your life *today.* I wrote about this at length in my book *Messages from Spirit* in the section on oracle abuse.) It's so important to not get ahead of yourself. You also have to resolve your past issues so that you're not constantly re-traumatizing yourself, or second-guessing whether you should have done things differently.

As spiritual beings temporarily having a human experience, we've chosen to live within time . . . to perceive that there is a past, present, and future. These categories of experience can be helpful for understanding our lives and healing ourselves, but it's also very helpful to understand the true nature and shape of time.

The Shape of Time

While we all learned in elementary school to draw timelines from left to right, with long-ago events recorded on the left and more recent ones farther to the right, time is not arranged in a straight line. In fact, at the smallest level of reality that we can identify, the quantum scale, it isn't linear or even very logical, but rather surreal. The rules of linear time don't exist, because linear time is a construct of our rational mind. Nature's time is very different.

Let go of the mental image of a timeline, and instead imagine time as a coil or three-dimensional spiral that begins with the past and moves you into the future as you travel farther along. A spiral is a line that loops back around to the same point. In fact, imagine that historical timeline from the fifth grade turned into a coil with no beginning and no ending. You'll notice that the conditions of war come back around, as do those for social movements. History repeats itself, and everything old is new again. This is how time works.

In Gregg Braden's fascinating book *Fractal Time,* he discusses at length the way in which conditions repeat in all of our lives, both collectively and individually, in a fractal pattern. A fractal is a shape that contains smaller versions of the same shape, such as a square made up of other, smaller squares. Fractals can be found everywhere in nature, from the arrangement of a flower's petals to the structure of ice crystals. Fractal time repeats previous conditions. Similarly, seasons cycle around, and while one spring is never exactly the same as the others, each spring has certain conditions you can count on.

Because time is a spiral or fractal, and we cycle back to previous conditions, we're reissued an invitation to any event we missed the first time around. This gives us the chance to "get it right" at last. It explains why circumstances of our lives repeat themselves and why, if we change our perceptions and behaviors, we're able to experience those circumstances with less suffering when they recur. We don't have to answer the call to begin another unfulfilling relationship with an unavailable partner, or carry on the same old conflict with a sibling.

In fractal time, each part mirrors the whole, in the same way the twigs on a tree mimic the shape of the branch, which mimics the shape of the tree itself. And in fractal time, endings mirror beginnings. Gregg points out that the dire forecasts for the end of an era of human experience is slated for December 21, 2012, and yet that day also marks the beginning of a *new* era. This isn't the first time that our planet has experienced this shift in ages. According to the scientific data on the physical age of the earth, we've been here before and survived! The civilization of Atlantis may have been lost, but we have more information now and have the ability and awareness to choose to experience this monumental shift with greater benefits for all of life.

Working with fractal time allows us to recognize that with death comes new opportunities for life; with loss comes gain. When we forget this truth about the nature of time, we begin to feel lost, because we can't see the cycles, patterns, and hope for creating something better. Remember, we're microcosmic versions of what's happening to the greater collective, so we needn't be so overwhelmed with the global story. We can focus on our responsibility to be mindful in our own lives. As Gandhi said, we need to be the change we want to see in the world—one person, belief, thought, prayer, and action at a time. We can't change the cycles, but we can change our reactions to them.

In nature, the seasons and cycles teach us about predictability, to trust that what dies in winter will be reborn, and that what is planted in the spring will yield fruit in the fall. That's why when you find yourself in the Frozen Land, you can feel confident that in time all will melt. First, however, something must die, and you have the opportunity to use this time in this land to "ice" your anger or conflict and, ultimately, let go of what no longer serves you.

The Frozen Land

Sometimes, our emotional reality is so harsh that we shut down and become numb. We enter the Frozen Land, where time seems to stand still and the heat of our anger, fear, jealousy, or sadness is cooled. We "put things on ice" and have a chance to rest.

The Frozen Land may seem harsh at first, but then you become acclimated to the cold. As you walk around, you notice the beauty of the place: the light captured in icicles that encase the twigs and branches of trees. Everything is still and quiet, and your furious thoughts have calmed down. And yet, like most of us, you probably greet the Frozen Land with resistance. You'd rather "do" something to fix your situation—*now*.

The Spirit of the Frozen Land is always available to show you around. She will explain that winter is a season that will inevitably turn to spring. The Frozen Land will then seem to disappear, but it will only do so in *your* reality, for this is a magical and eternal place that many will visit.

The Frozen Land isn't somewhere to stay, nor would you want to. Only the oracle of the landscape, the Spirit of this frigid place, can remain here in the icy environment. She will guide you to a cold, dark crystal cave where you can take a long winter's nap and dream new dreams for your life. She'll explain that there is nothing you can do right now because it is time for all to sleep, but that your emotions will eventually rekindle and you'll find yourself someplace else. In the meantime, she'll ask you whether there's something in your life that needs to die here so that spring may come again.

Harsh though the land may seem, you'll find that it can be refreshing as it restores your sense of self and puts you back into your body. Whatever is troubling you, you can thaw it out later. For now, sleep. Heal. Regenerate. And dream.

The Frozen Land is a place of surrender. Someday, you may consciously choose to go there and allow time to stand still.

Slowing the Pace of Time

The cycles of nature also teach the lesson of patience. There's no rushing the first buds of spring. They will burst forth into blossom and bloom when it's the right time and not a moment sooner, so there's no point in trying to move things along.

In fact, when you relax into the seasons of your life, you truly enjoy living as a single person, being at the height of your career, or parenting young children. You take things as they come instead of forcing life to conform to your timetable. Then it's less frustrating when the same old situation cycles around again, and you remember your power to magically transform it.

Slowing down actually gives you *more* access to time. I find that when I'm in the Sticky Swamp, there's no opening in my schedule to do anything, and my to-do list becomes a huge ogre that threatens to swallow me whole. If I'm getting ready for my radio show, I'm worried about writing up an e-course; and if I'm writing up an e-course, I'm thinking about how I had to postpone a meeting with my friends; and now that I'm doing that on Thursday, I'll never finish up that other project I was going to get done by the weekend . . . blah, blah, blah. Time collapses as my mind does a hopscotch through past, present, and future; and then I feel lost. *When am I?*

However, if I spend 20 minutes meditating on the present moment and counting my breaths, which is my favorite mindfulness practice, I use my magic to expand time, which makes room for the sacred work I do. I come back to my everyday consciousness knowing that *all* the work I do is sacred, and there's time and space for everything now that I've slowed down. Maybe that's an illusion, but it's a convincing one! Somehow, it seems that I'm able to go from the twig to the branch, the little square to the big one, and everything that has to get done gets done. Whatever *doesn't* get done, I don't worry about.

When you hopscotch from past to future to present to past, and back again, you end up rushing time. Then it takes forever to get anything done because you're frittering away the hours worrying, venting, procrastinating, and wishing for what might be instead of staying in the present, making it happen. This is when time feels like it begins to speed up and contract. The more you affirm that there's no time, the less of it there is.

Slow time and you find the clarity to see that the way out of the Sticky Swamp is to ease up, prioritize, and then do something practical and simple. Multitasking is a great thing, but not when it becomes an addiction and you're actually considering texting while driving or some other madness. When you're going too quickly, you don't have time for being fully present in any given task, and that lands you back in those difficult emotional landscapes. You ignore all the big red flags that say, *This person is not on the up-and-up,* because you just want to get things done—and whoops, what you didn't have the luxury of dealing with is now going to end up taking far more of your time and energy.

Altering the Map of the Past

Slow down, and allow your perception to begin to change. Soon you'll find that your past, and the Map, is altered. You'll look back at your interactions with someone who once persecuted you, and may remember what it felt like to be perched on a cliff above sharp rocks, unable to step back from the accusations and abuse, afraid of losing your footing. Back then, you wished you could get around this monstrously strong creature who had you trapped and on the edge.

However, as you come to heal the beliefs that caused you to engage in this precarious standoff, you won't remember those conflicts in the same way. Instead, you may feel that in those days, it was as if you were on the bank of a Raging River, calling across it to tell this individual how you felt while he stood on the other bank, unaware of your presence, unable to hear what you had to say. The sense of danger you used to feel around that person will have given way to irritation, or even sadness as you think about how futile your efforts were, how much energy you wasted trying to get through to him.

Someday when you revisit that time in your life, you'll experience the banks of the Raging River without frustration, because you'll no longer feel trapped. You'll know you're only there temporarily. Or, you may end up in the Canyon of Echoes whenever you think back to the past, and you can use this opportunity to change your perceptions and beliefs by putting a new message "out there" and letting it reverberate.

Often when people leave my weekend intensive in Sedona, they've acquired a new vision of the past, which magically alters their vantage point on their journey forward. The weekend process begins with a ritual on Friday evening in which participants are guided into a new way of perceiving themselves that entails entering into a magical realm of self-discovery. The entire weekend is performed as a sacred ceremony, beginning with anointing oils, a water ritual with special bath salts, and a meditation to incubate a dream that will help them begin their new journey.

Over the next two days, I guide the participants through a number of powerful processes designed to orient them to their personal Maps and help them discover who they've been listening to and what they need to shift within themselves in order to progress. We look closely at what the repetitive landscapes, allies, and challengers have to "say" about their beliefs and attitudes about the past and how that has impeded their ability to manifest their purpose, prosperity, and full creative expression of themselves. I then lead everyone into a profound and transformative process of redirecting their point of view.

Having had a *Shazam!* moment, they find when they return home that their story has been rewritten now that their hearts have been given space to heal. They discover that new opportunities suddenly appear to come alive when they affirm that surrendering to "what was" changes the present and opens new pathways to the future.

Knowing that you have the power to choose your perception is like having a magic wand in your hand that allows you to shift time.

Memories That Shift or Reappear

Oddly enough, when your perception changes, it not only magically transforms your memories of the lands you traversed years ago, but it awakens new memories that match up with your new perception.

When I was younger, I saw my mother as my victimizer, as a person whose tone of voice alone could send me straight to a battlefield. There, I would flail about in terror and anger, blinded by cannon smoke that billowed up around me.

Now that I'm older and have done a lot of work on myself, I can look back on my mother and see her behaviors very differently. I know that as a Holocaust survivor, she carried pain and fear that darkened her thoughts and too often prevented her from expressing kindness, affection, and compassion toward her daughter. I also see how difficult it must have been for her to experience the intrusive quality of my gift (I wrote about this in my first book, *Remembering the Future*) and how painful it was for her to watch my self-destruction through alcoholism. She was powerless to rescue me.

I've healed my relationship with my mother now that she's gone because I have a greater respect and appreciation for her. As a result, I've now regained old memories that my mind had long buried in a dark cupboard away from my conscious mind, memories that didn't match up with my image of myself as a victim of a mother who didn't treat me right. I respect, understand, and love her unreservedly now.

I now see that when my mother took me to the hospital after I was raped, and swore me to silence, she did it to protect me, not to stop me from hurting the family. She'd been through an identical experience during the war, and she was trying to help me be strong and not give my power away to the pain and shame of that experience. She held my hand in the emergency room and cried. It wasn't for herself alone that she cried; it was for me, too. Her anger was directed at the horrific situation; and she rightly feared revisiting a painful, personal memory of her own. At the time I could only see that she was ashamed of me because of my own unbridled self-centeredness, which had caused me to take a risk that led to the rape.

This memory and the subsequent new insight could only rise into my consciousness after I gave up my story of "Poor Beleaguered Me," and I couldn't give up that story until I revisited that battlefield and learned the lesson of the place. Only then did I see that the smoke had cleared and I wasn't confronting *her* on this battlefield after all: I was my own opponent. So I certainly didn't need to be wasting my energy fighting my mom and aching from the burden of wearing that heavy suit of armor.

The sad part is that I couldn't see all of this while she was alive. I was able to face my part in our dynamic only years after she had passed over. I began to remember the past differently.

Our memories are remarkably selective. That's why feuds can begin when one family member remembers Dad and Mom, life in the childhood home, or a particular event completely differently from how everyone else does. Even in the moment when an event occurs, our minds can distort our perception dramatically to make it match up with our overall beliefs about ourselves, others, and the world around us. Add the passing of time, and memories become even more unreliable.

We can get lost in the details of our memories, but if we delve into the Map, we recognize the emotional experience and learn what we can from it, which allows us to leave it in the past. Otherwise, we're simply sketching in every detail of the landscape we're trapped in, and we run the risk of getting stuck in this harsh terrain, reliving those painful memories and emotions.

Step into a New Past, Present, and Future

So when you begin to observe cycles that seem to repeat in your life, they're invitations to do things differently this time around. It takes the magic of mindfulness not to be reactive and give in to the old comfortable habits, but even the greatest wizards have to practice their magic. The following exercise will help you begin working with your Map.

Exercise: Where and When Am I?

This exercise has two parts: (1) the In-Vizion process for discovering your current landscape; and (2) a journaling prompt to explore and record your relationship to this land: where you are; why you're here; and whether you're dwelling in the past, present, or future.

Step 1: The In-Vizion Process

Unlike with a guided visualization, this process is one that requires you to let your soul reach into your subconscious mind to tell you about your surroundings and your emotional experiences. This is active dreaming, asking your soul to translate the stories locked away inside you by inspiring your imagination to paint the picture with symbols. Sit quietly, letting the thoughts in your mind settle down or fade in volume as you focus on your breathing. Then ask yourself:

Where am I?

Allow your inner awareness to show you the landscape and all its features. Be there without judgment. Don't slip into analyzing the place. Just notice where you are and how you feel.

Step 2: Journaling

In a journal, write your answers to these questions:

- So, where are you? What is your inner landscape?

- Have you been here before?

- When are you? Are you in the future, thinking about what might be? Or are you in the past, remembering?

- Do you feel positive emotions in this landscape, or negative ones?

- Is there a lesson to be learned here?

- Is there something to be gained by visiting this place?

- Have you been here a lot?

- Does it feel as if you keep coming back here for no reason?

- How can the experience of being in this particular landscape temporarily help you in your life today?

When you let go of the habit of running away from your present emotional state, you start to find the courage to face the difficult memories of the past and the harsh realities of the future that you may have to confront given the parameters of your personal history. In upcoming chapters, you'll learn more about the allies who can help you on your journey; as well as the magical tools, such as talismans and medicine bags, that can embolden you.

But first you must learn the dangers of entering the Ghost-lands that we all move into when we linger too long in the past or the future. There are secrets to escaping them, as you shall see.

Traveler's Notes

- Part of the reason we feel lost is because we think too much about the past or future instead of the present moment.

- We're very likely to avoid the present when we're in an emotionally distressing situation.

- If we avoid our emotions, we find ourselves back in the same old emotional place again and again.

- When we consciously interact with the Map, we're less likely to find ourselves in distressing emotional landscapes, and when we do enter them, we're aware that we're not prisoners and are able to leave much sooner.

- Time is a fractal or spiral. Whatever you experience will come around again in some form.

- The Frozen Land is a place you go when you must "put things on ice," rest, and reflect before taking action.

- Slowing down and becoming mindful actually creates more time for you.

- When you shift your perception of the past, the Map changes, and you even recall memories you'd long forgotten because they didn't match up with the story you've always told about your life.

Chapter Three

LOST IN THE GHOSTLANDS

"In the equation that is life on Earth, your future grows shorter each year and your past elongates, fills, swells . . . even a bad past can feel safer than the present because at least past horrors are <u>known</u>— it shimmers in a warm if slightly unreal glow. We can't airbrush the present."

— ANNELI RUFUS

"Having spent the better part of my life trying either to relive the past or experience the future before it arrives, I have come to believe that in between these two extremes is peace."

— AUTHOR UNKNOWN

Have you ever gotten lost in wishful thinking, in the fog of a fantasy future where images tantalize you but refuse to hold still and manifest into reality?

Any land can be rendered a Ghostland if you linger there too long. In a Ghostland, no emotional growth or healing occurs. You freeze time instead of moving through this landscape and into the next. Because it's only your mind, not your true emotional experience, which is keeping you here, the color, texture, and reality of the place are drained. All is translucent and without substance—including you—because you're in a ghostly place. You wander through it, confused, lost, and outside of time, until you snap out of it and let yourself *feel* your difficult emotions.

Ghostlands of the Past

When the answer to the question *When are you?* is: *Back in my past—again,* you have an opportunity to learn the lessons of the land. The strong emotions you feel in this traumatic locale inspire you to do the work of learning and growth, painful though your transformation may be. If you stay and look around, you'll eventually discover the wisdom that will help you escape the next time you end up here.

But a Ghostland is not a place of strong, true emotions; it's a place of obsession where you artificially revive old emotions and relive something that is already past. Is there something in your past you fixate on even though there's nothing to be gained from your constantly thinking and talking about it? Is there an event or relationship you continually ruminate about? Do you find that your attraction to your ex-partner is long gone, but your anger about how he should have done this or you should have done that keeps flaring up as you replay in your mind the scenes of your relationship?

The regrets of loss are transformative, and you'll feel them when you're in the Valley of Loss, but the regrets in Ghostlands of the past are, like the land itself, without substance. You don't feel genuine remorse; there is no real pain to inspire growth. Instead, you simply think and think and think about what you could have done differently and cause yourself to manufacture emotions as a result of your obsession. You conjure up resentments that are ghosts of old hurts to keep you company—three ghosts, to be exact, who insist on following you around. Their names are Shoulda, Woulda, and Coulda. I'm sure you've met them in their ghostly goblin forms, not quite real, yet not easily dismissed.

No new nugget of information is going to reveal itself if you keep turning over the events of the past in the hopes of mining some gem. Instead, whatever thoughts you form about this experience will be ethereal and ghostlike, floating about instead of becoming rooted in you as wisdom.

For example, in a Ghostland of the past, you might have the insight: *I don't have to listen to people who want to drag me back into cynicism.* These are wise words, but in a Ghostland, they remain mere words, without form. For them to have the potential to help you stop re-traumatizing yourself, they have to have substance for you. They have to become a part of your awareness, embedded in your heart and not just your head. This can only happen if you allow yourself to feel your true emotions, get back into a genuine landscape on the Map, and do the work you need to do. Learning the lesson requires that you begin *living* it.

Nostalgia and Romanticism

Another way you can end up in a Ghostland of the past is through romanticism.

Giving in to nostalgia now and again is healthy. It rekindles feelings of happiness, and when you're in a place of challenge, it's good to take yourself on a mini-vacation to the lovely lands you've visited. Nostalgia fills you with joy and enthusiasm that becomes a part of your present, if you let it. Close your eyes and think about one of your favorite memories for a few moments. Relive it. Do you feel its magic filling you in the present? Nostalgia gets you thinking about how you can make yourself happier right now and in the future—at least, that is its purpose.

It's like when the Ghost of Christmas Past took Scrooge by the hand and showed him the scenes from his childhood. Grouchy old Scrooge's demeanor completely changed as he delighted in the sight of his beloved sister, alive and young again. But then he was reminded of his nephew, whose kind overtures he had rebuffed in the present day. You can visit the happy scenes of the past and relish the wonderful emotions your nostalgia re-creates in you, but you can't live there.

Romanticism happens when you practice selective memory and forget the suffering, the shadow that always accompanies the light. You stop thinking about how you can bring happiness into your life today and tomorrow and instead dwell in a past viewed through rose-colored glasses. The good old days were never really as good as you'd like to think they were.

Romanticism can become addictive. In *Harry Potter and the Sorcerer's Stone*, the orphaned wizard discovers an enchanted mirror where he can see what he most desires: his parents alive, smiling and waving at him. Professor Dumbledore has to rescue Harry from this dangerous magical object; he explains that many a wizard has gotten lost for years gazing at what he desired. Time stops when you obsess, and you wander that Ghostland of romanticism.

Living in the past doesn't give you any emotional nourishment or sense of purpose in the present. The more you dwell there, the more time gets away from you and you feel lost and not in control. Your life essence slowly seeps away from your core until you become a ghost yourself. So while it takes courage to surrender to the present, it's the only way to begin creating a better future. The magic is restored when you ask, *Does this issue have true substance today?*

Ghostlands of the Future

When you fixate on times to come, you can find yourself in a seductive Ghostland that beckons with both "large promise and poor performance," as they say in 12-step programs. Remember, the future isn't solid. Often clients tell me that they had a reading from a psychic who saw something in their future that upset them, and they want to know if they have the power to change the path they're on. Of course they do!

Intuition and prescient insights about what will take place should empower people, not make them afraid. I believe the future can be changed even by the very fact that we can observe its potentials and possibilities. Back when I was drinking, another psychic told me that I would experience years and years of unhappiness and would never get married. Well, I got sober the following year, and I have a very happy marriage! Yet, had I stayed in the landscape I was in and not made any changes in my life, her prediction might very well have come true.

Even without predictions from a seer, people can talk themselves into feeling fear, anger, and sadness when they think something awful will happen to them. To avoid these feelings, they try to convince themselves that the future only holds good news for them—and that anything challenging they come across they'll be able to handle because they've got it all figured out.

You might script a whole story about how your life will unfold because of this or that. Yet you can't control the future; you can change your "now," where that future is seeded. When you buy into the illusion that you *can* control it, you end up in a Ghostland.

Contemplating potential problems and allowing yourself to feel how awful they would be could be a helpful exercise if you were to do it consciously and follow up by thoughtfully considering your next move and taking action. The challenge in doing so is to avoid working yourself into a state of distress, which puts you into a difficult landscape—say, that of the Immovable Mountain, which stands in your way; or the Valley of Loss. But at least there's a chance you'll learn something there. In a Ghostland, no learning, emotion, or action takes place. You simply become overwhelmed with pessimistic thoughts and trying to figure out how to avoid pain, or you're fixated on arriving at the magical destination where there are no problems to be solved.

The mind can foolishly convince itself that the more information it has, the easier it will be to skirt any unpleasantness or danger that lies ahead. It can also very efficiently find all the reasons why something will never work. You decide there's no point in trying to change anything, and get a certain comfort from the belief that you don't have to risk suffering. After thinking about all the many ways you might avoid disaster, you decide to do nothing and simply hope that nothing changes. Then you wander the Ghostlands until life changes all on its own and you're sent to a painful emotional landscape after all.

At this time in our planet's evolving story, it's particularly important to recognize that stability and peace must come from within, since so much that is changing in the world at large is affecting us as individuals. It's all part of the evolution we're experiencing. Mindfully bringing yourself back into your awareness allows you to enter a new landscape and leave behind the one with no substance. Whenever you're in the Ghostlands, you're lost. But you can always find the treasure of your self in present time.

If you were to ask the Spirit of the Ghostland what gift can be found here, his answer would be simple. There is one question you must ask yourself in order to experience an abracadabra, *Shazam!* moment: *Does this condition I'm thinking of have true substance?* If you see no evidence that gives form to your thoughts here and now in this very moment, then you must seek your escape.

Escaping and Avoiding the Ghostlands

The way out of the Ghostlands is to walk between two pillars: *surrendered acceptance* and *creative action.* You accept that you're not the only mapmaker and that there are parameters to any enchanted Map, and you act as a co-creator of your life, working with Spirit. You accept that the past is gone and you aren't the sole force in charge of your future, and you take responsibility for making changes rather than waiting for someone to rescue you.

By walking through these two pillars, you'll put yourself back to where you're meant to be in time. You'll no longer spend countless hours wondering whether you'll win the heart of the man you want; instead, you'll surrender to what is true now. You'll no longer wait until your perfect life arrives according to your specifications; rather, you'll live your best life now. You'll leave your resentments behind after seeing your part in keeping them alive now.

It's possible to avoid the Ghostlands if you're mindful of how to contemplate the past and future in healthy ways. If you'd like to experience nostalgia, enjoy the memories for a bit, but then turn yourself to the present. Are you creating new, even better, memories now? If not, how can you do so? The best way to work with the future is to visualize your life filled with abundance, security, love, and all the good things you long for and then take action in the present. Act as if the future you're envisioning is already here, as if this scene is true. Claim your highest good now, not later on. Imagine yourself into a state of peace and calm, of joy or excitement.

By exercising the power of your imagination, you can actually train your brain to become used to feeling good . . . which, if you're used to feeling bad, can seem like a miraculous change.

You get to enjoy basking in positive emotions that your fantasies generate, and you become inspired to make the future happen today. The primary environment you inhabit is that of your thoughts, feelings, and beliefs; and you're really experiencing it *now*—not yesterday, not tomorrow. Personally, I love to work with dream boards and pictures, and enjoy all that I'm aiming to attain for myself as if it were a current reality. It's inspiring and energizing, and makes me feel excited and hopeful—and it actually produces results. The more you claim your intention now, the truer it becomes in your outer world.

My clients often ask me, "What is my purpose? How do I serve, and what will really make me happy?" When you imagine your future, and what your own purpose and goals might be, you'll get in touch with all the many emotions you would experience if that future were true today. You may realize that you should alter your goal given that you'd love to have a particular career, for instance, but not enough to have to move to another part of the country or give up something valuable in your current circumstances to pursue that particular dream.

Also, you can look to the future and imagine the process of achieving your goal. This is important, since it's rare to see the things you want accompanied by the hard work or sacrifices that go along with them. Do you want to be an "author," or do you want to actually put pen to paper and write a book? Do you want to be a healer if it involves a long apprenticeship?

Regardless of the goal, you must create the emotional reality of those future circumstances within yourself in order for the external world to begin reflecting your new inner reality. Then you must be open to the way the dream manifests.

Dreams can become obsessions when you start to overlook all the other possibilities before you because you're attached to what you'd envisioned. You may think you planted starflowers in your Field of Dreams, but how will you feel if the seedlings turn into sunflowers instead? To nurture those flowers, you may have to let your original dream die, but what replaces it may yield something far more marvelous than you could have imagined. Affirm: "I am living my best life now, allowing the Divine plan for me to unfold perfectly," and open to what Spirit brings.

If you spend too much time in a fantasy of the future, two things are likely to happen: (1) you'll get caught running between a Ghostland of the future that eludes you and a landscape of suffering caused by your attachment to a particular outcome; and (2) you won't attend to what you can do today to make that future happen.

As an aspiring recording artist, I was desperate to get that big record deal that would rescue me from obscurity and bring me a sense of value and importance (or so I imagined), and I felt frustrated and resentful when it didn't happen for me in the time frame I wanted it to. In retrospect, I could have stopped worrying about how I was going to land that deal and instead focus on improving my guitar-playing skills and work even more on my craft.

While I was obsessed with getting the deal, I wasn't able to be fully present in the "now," and the painful truth was obvious; however, I couldn't reconcile my fantasy with what was really going on. I got everything I wanted eventually, right down to the name of the record label I placed on my dream board, but only after I had given up the relentless ambition and surrendered to the path as it was revealed a day at a time.

In a reading, I might tell you that I see you on a stage someday, teaching something of value to others, but that's not going to be a reality if you sit around dreaming of how wonderful that will feel and do nothing practical to make it happen. Wishful thinking blinds you to what opportunities are available to you today.

Envision the future, yes, but set it in motion in the present. Be patient and always remain in a state of detachment, letting the proverbial arrow fly through the air of its own accord. You're not the wind that carries it there, but you must be the one to shoot it. Your dream may also have some surprising characteristics that you weren't considering. You might need to do research on what it would be like to experience the circumstances you're trying to bring about. The following exercise will help you get clarity on how to leave the Ghostland of wishful thinking and make your time-traveling to the future more effective.

Exercise: Envisioning the Future

As you immerse yourself in envisioning your future, let go of the fantasy you've created for yourself for now. Take out your journal and ask yourself these questions to find out where you are in relation to where you want to be. This is a fact-finding exercise, not one that should be approached in a judgmental way. Always approach self-discovery with compassion.

- "What does my heart tell me is my purpose? Do I know, or am I still discovering the answer? What have I come to know about this so far?"

- "Does it feel as if Spirit has plans for me that I'm turning a blind eye to? How can I describe this feeling? How do I know?"

- "Am I able to bring a fulfilling vision of the future into the now by beginning down the path toward it? Do I resist this journey because it feels more comfortable to remain in wishful thinking?"

- "Am I afraid of achieving this goal and living this life I envision? Is fear holding me back in any way? If so, what is my fear?"

- "Should I make peace with this fear so that it subsides, or should I explore it further? What feels right?"

- "Do I need to research what this experience would be like rather than guessing at it? How might I begin researching it?"

- "Am I fixated on the future and squinting to see the details rather than starting the wheels in motion today? What could I do today to begin bringing this vision into reality?"

- "Am I feeling unsure of what to do? Do I need to meditate, surrender to Spirit, and let the next step on the path reveal itself?"

When obsessing about the ideal future causes you to miss your opportunities today, you have to be patient and wait for them to come around again. Otherwise, you end up struggling to make it happen because you didn't work with Divine timing. Spirit put the boat and the oars at the dock, but you didn't get around to walking over to it because you were too busy daydreaming about how great it would be once you'd already rowed downstream to the Golden Palace of Wealth, the Resting Tree, Easy Street, or another landscape you long to visit. Now the sun has set, the waters are choppy, and you'll have to wait.

If you stay in your head and avoid action, as well as the difficult emotions you might experience if you were to take some risk, you turn those places you wish to visit into Ghostlands. You can look, but you can't touch . . . because it's all a mirage.

One of my clients, Joel, was putting together a business deal with a friend and told me he was frustrated and unhappy. He explained that he and his friend had plenty of grandiose schemes to launch an innovative product, but the project wasn't getting off the ground because they were bickering over the proverbial pieces of the pie. I asked him to imagine that he and his partner were famous explorers having a business meeting about a new venture. I knew that if I had him set the stage and replace the players with characters, he would observe what he couldn't see when caught up in his emotions.

A week later, Joel called me and told me the story he had imagined. He was Christopher Columbus, his business partner was his first mate, and they were in a tavern scheming about what they would discover in the New World. (Granted, the real Columbus didn't know he was going to "discover" the New World, let alone anything in it, but your imaginings don't have to be historically accurate.) They were sitting in a private alcove, poring over roughly drawn maps, whispering excitedly of places they would conquer and the gold they would find.

As they reveled in their glory, they got increasingly drunk on alcohol and dreams of great riches. They began to argue about who would lay claim to a particular piece of land, then got into a fistfight and were thrown out of the tavern in the pouring rain. The two men had no money and couldn't pay their bill. They also had no boat, no crew, and no queen to sponsor their trip. Imagine if all they ever did was drink and scheme and talk about the fantasy and never found a way to do all the legwork to launch their journey?

After he had created this fable in parallel to his current situation, Joel was able to get beyond his frustration with his partner and acknowledge his own role in their endless sparring. He was able to implement changes with his partner by shifting their focus from the future to the now and identifying what he himself could do differently. By using his imagination to create a scenario that matched his emotions, he found that it was possible to be honest with himself about the role he was playing in this conflict—and he was able to see what was going to happen if he continued to act the same way.

Think about how many plans are made by armchair astronauts who never reach liftoff. If you want to reach for the stars, you must at the very least leave your house!

Faith in What Will Come to Be

Ground your dreams by planting seeds in the Field of Dreams and nurturing them. You "scatter" them all the time when you live your life without focus or self-evaluation. Are they falling on fertile ground . . . or on rock? Do you know what you've planted . . . and what you're tending? And what about the quality of the soil? Your emotions and unconscious beliefs will provide the nourishment for your seeds. How will you cultivate anything in a soil made of fear or an overriding need to control? The quality of what you create will be greatly influenced by the environment in which your dreams are planted.

And are you afraid to sow a seed with intention because you're worried it might not grow—or maybe even that it *might* and you'd face difficulties or responsibilities as a result?

Of course you can't know all the intricacies of why some things grow and others don't. You simply have to surrender to the mystery and have faith. There is order in the world even in what appears to be chaos. The universe is aware and conscious, creating and changing constantly. Act as if you trust Spirit and you'll see evidence of Divine Intelligence and order everywhere. I know that's not so easy, but hold on to your compass and remember that Spirit will be with you, always.

When I first stopped drinking, I couldn't imagine how I was going to function, let alone be happy, without alcohol. I couldn't imagine what my life would be. It wasn't just that I was giving up my drug of choice; I was also giving up friends who wouldn't want to be around me if I wasn't drinking, and opportunities to bond over a bottle of wine with someone in the record business. Who would I be without the bottle? Who would want to hang out with me, or start a conversation with me? I was afraid of myself and believed that without my crutch I would be unwanted and unworthy and left out of life . . . and of love.

Looking back, I can see how irrational my fears were. Drinking had led me to make a terrible mess of my life. Of course, things would get better, and I was someone other than Colette, the girl who can knock back a shot of tequila like nobody's business and party all night. But I couldn't see that at the time. I had to hit Rock Bottom to find the courage to embrace the mystery and let God figure out the details of how I was going to get to a place of tranquility and joy. I had to trust in the possibilities that had yet to present themselves. There were seedlings I was unaware of; I'd overlooked them while I stood desperately over a barren patch calling, "Grow something already!"

I had to be willing to let Spirit decide which seeds would grow. I had nowhere else to turn. I couldn't live the way I was living anymore and had no clue about what was ahead, so I surrendered absolutely and found my compass. By trusting in the possibility that Spirit had plans for me that were yet unseen, I opened myself up to them.

How do you build up this trust and faith? You have to see yourself clearly as you are, know the truth about your circumstances, and break out of denial. No matter what the temporary conditions of your life are, even if you believe they're permanent, you have to honor what you have now in the present and be grateful for it. Gratitude and humility open the doors of possibility. You don't have to fall down or fall apart to find faith and trust in Spirit. You can do that now! Then you'll get an inkling of what your life might be like if you were deeply happy in your new circumstances, whatever they are.

You have to heal yourself in the present and find the beauty in your life today, no matter how ugly or bleak your current landscape may seem. I now look back at that Barren Desert I was in so much of the time when I was drinking, and I see it differently. I see the potential for life, the seedlings I could have nourished had I not been so focused on the cracked earth and the succulent fruits I thought "ought" to be there for me.

And in the magical desert, there is resilience and survival and an urge for resourcefulness even if it means digging deep for water until your hands bleed. Life's magic is everywhere, even in places that make it hard to believe. Learn better navigation skills and you'll find it easier to tolerate the challenging landscapes and prevent yourself from wandering the Ghostlands, out of time and avoiding the healing and growth you're meant to experience.

Traveler's Notes

- If your thoughts are constantly focused on the past or future instead of the present, you're experiencing a Ghostland.

- In a Ghostland, there is no learning or growth because you get stuck inside your mind.

- The only way out of an emotional Ghostland is to allow yourself to feel and identify your emotions.

- An obsession with the past can take the form of fruitless nostalgia that prevents you from experiencing joy in the present and planning for something better in the future.

- Dwelling on the past can involve regret that remains a thought about what "should" have happened instead of becoming a key to discovering the valuable lesson of the experience.

- An obsession with the future may be wishful thinking, which prevents you from discovering what you can do today to manifest your dream . . . and then doing it.

- Speculating about the future may involve fear and dread. You must surrender to Spirit to get out of this Ghostland.

Part 11

NAVIGATIONAL
HELP ON
YOUR MAP

Chapter Four

WHO IS GUIDING YOU?

> *"It's not what you are that holds you back,*
> *it's what you think you are not."*
>
> — DENIS WAITLEY

> *"If you hear a voice within you say 'you cannot paint,'*
> *then by all means paint . . . and that voice will be silenced."*
>
> — VINCENT VAN GOGH

Who are you listening to?

Is it the voice of your emotions? Your thoughts?

Is it your intuition speaking?

Is this a voice of wisdom . . . or a voice of deception?

I'm sure you've heard that you should listen to your inner knowing, but that's difficult to do when that wise input can easily be masked by other voices within you that aren't going to guide you well on your journey. Your task is to sort out what these voices are, their messages, and the quality of their advice. You can learn to distinguish between the voice of truth and that of the trickster and enjoy the assistance of the allies within who are always there for you, eager to make your adventure rich and wondrous.

The Loudest Voices Within

The voices of your thoughts and beliefs, which often become impassioned, can be so loud and incessant that they distract you from the quieter voices inside you. The greatest wisdom and most valuable insights and guidance are whispered, barely audible underneath the cacophony of your ego.

You've probably been told not to listen to the ego because if you do, you'll cause suffering for yourself. Yet like everything else in nature, the ego exists for a reason. It is the very loud voice of the survival instinct, telling you what you have to do to ensure your safety and to protect your sense of self. It is also the voice of your personality and individuality, the self that is a unique expression of your Divine soul. You love your partner's sense of humor and ability to be hopeful in the most trying of circumstances, and your best friend's sincere dedication to her craft as an artist, as well as her loyalty. You love what the "ego" is in others, so why would you fear, dislike, or dismiss your own?

There is a part of your ego that is healthy, and perhaps a part that is wounded. To love and appreciate who you are as an individual moving across your Map is psychologically healthy. And when faced with genuine danger, you *need* to have a survival instinct, a sense of your life as something valuable and worthy of protection. This instinct is an important part of the ego.

The problem is when your ego convinces you that the *only* thing that matters is the survival of you as one individual human being. It is this fear that causes you to believe that the world is a scary place that doesn't support your well-being, so you'd better impose your beliefs on others and take what you can get—quickly—before someone else does.

Every one of us is going to get hurt, suffer illness, be betrayed by someone, lose loved ones, and experience the death of the physical body at some point. The ego, understandably, wants to deny that painful reality. When it can't, it often makes too much of a situation, because it's constantly seeing evidence of threat and danger. The ego reasons that one bad relationship is evidence that all relationships will fail for you and cause you pain, so it's best to avoid them, or try to manipulate them through dishonesty. You begin to expect, without even knowing it consciously, that the world will be filled with repetitive experiences.

When you're mostly identifying with your eternal, sacred nature, you see yourself as a magical soul entwined with the Divine matrix. Then you're able to accept the more upsetting aspects of the human condition and not see losses and betrayals as evidence that you're in danger of annihilation. You operate from a higher level than the ego, which is dominated by fear and defensiveness. When you're oblivious to this higher nature, you see this planet as one frightening place. No wonder you can become hyper-vigilant about protecting yourself.

It's not easy to surrender to the mystery of the Map and its unknown territories. Of course you wish you could be the only mapmaker and be able to control everything and protect yourself from pain. Your ego self is afraid of being hurt, pushed aside, or even ignored completely as you identify with your soul self, a co-creator that is able to surrender to Spirit. The ego feels it needs to make a racket to keep your attention. That's when your intuition, which allows you to hear the voice of your soul, gets drowned out.

Fortunately, you can learn to adjust the volume on these distracting voices. You can observe the voice of your ego and learn what you can from it, yet not let it speak so loudly that your intuition can't be heard.

It's challenging to work with our egos. They are very sensitive. In fact, the word *ego* itself makes many people feel immediately defensive—"What? I don't have an ego!"

The Goblin and Chatterbox are imaginary characters I've invented to help you get past this understandable resistance to looking at your ego's messages. Think of the Goblin as the trickster, which is the most troublesome and wounded aspect of your ego, and the Chatterbox as the benign aspect that distracts you with a lot of unnecessary thoughts. Both must be tamed, or quieted, for you to uncover the hidden wisdom that will guide you well. Learn to work with them and you can become your own oracle, receptive to the wisdom in the Divine matrix that you're a part of.

The Goblin

"Goblins are a different, more grotesque variety of gnomes. They are known to be playful, but at other times they are evil and their tricks could seriously harm people. A goblin smile curdles the blood and a laugh sours the milk and causes fruit to fall from the trees. They pester humans in a number of ways, such as hiding small objects, tipping over pails of milk and altering signposts. . . . They have no homes and usually live in mossy clefts in rocks and roots of ancient trees, although they never stay very long in the same place."

— MICHA F. LINDEMANS, *ENCYCLOPEDIA MYTHICA*

We fear the dark creatures in the woods and hiding in our closets. These are the Goblins, and they are born of our moments of suffering and develop into possessive hostage takers. They are mischievous tricksters who promise security, power, love, and happiness, enticing us to react to their messages of unworthiness and abandonment. And then they whisk us away to repetitive, troublesome, unrelenting inner landscapes.

Do you keep running into the same kind of difficult person who shows up in your life as if by some dark magic? Do you feel tested over and over on what appears to be the same issues, no matter how much work you feel you've done on yourself? Do you struggle with the behavior that comes from low self-worth? Do you judge others harshly? Do you act out compulsively even though you know that what you're doing isn't healthy? If so, you're being influenced by the trickster within you known as the Goblin.

The Goblin is the disowned part of yourself that's hiding somewhere in the darkest shadows within you. He is the source of your fear, pride, rage, lust, greed, procrastination, and other challenges in your character.

He represents the *shadow,* the archetypal label coined by Swiss psychologist Carl G. Jung. This shadow represents the universal experience of what we repress and disown about ourselves because these parts of the self make us uncomfortable.

Your Goblin is your wounded, fearful ego, the shadowy self that resides within your Map, making mischief or doing real harm as you struggle to keep hidden that which is unsightly, painful, or shameful. The Goblin represents the primary source of fear and all its subsequent by-products, such as anger, jealousy, defensiveness, and greed. He also represents the psychological issues you created when you didn't take in the lesson of your suffering because your pain was so great that you ran away from the landscape. He is the embodied voice of separation in all its forms.

Think of the Goblin as a type of gnome "gone wrong." In the 16th century, Swiss alchemist Paracelsus wrote of the gnome as a mythic creature representing the earth element whose job it was to protect treasure hidden underground. Gnomes symbolized the energy that protected the unformed potential within the world, and within oneself. Traditionally, gnomes couldn't come above the surface lest they be turned to stone as soon as they entered the light. Their job was to serve and guard things hidden beneath the earth, watching over seedlings and the gems of possibility yet to be mined.

But imagine that this now-homeless gnome has come up from underground and mutated, becoming a very active and naughty Goblin. Far from paralyzed once he's above ground, this little fellow really gets around and can be found in every unpleasant landscape—and he will show up in the more delightful ones as well, where he will trick you into leaving. Dispossessed, unloved, and unwanted, he will wreak havoc.

Imagine your inner landscape. Where might this deformed, sad troublemaker be hiding? Is it in a place that you try not to visit, a dark shadow of your awareness? You won't find the Goblin out in the open. He dances around at the roots of your Home Tree where lie your oldest memories of trauma, shame, worthlessness, repressed desire, rage, and social restrictions. You may not be able to find him right away, but you'll have no trouble seeing the results of his actions in your strong negative reactions to other people; in your grandiosity, lust, greed, pride, and self-centeredness; and in your fear and anger. You'll find your Goblin in the dark recesses of addiction and in the depths of hypocrisy. You'll find him wherever there is a secret. His is the voice that inflames your negative emotions and feelings of unworthiness.

The Goblin's Voice

Do you ever wonder if you're hearing the voice of your intuition or of your ego's fear? Is your Goblin lurking in your landscape, misguiding you? An intuitive feeling has a very different quality from a Goblin's declarations. He is relentlessly driven by fear, so his voice will stir up painful emotions in you. It will urge you to act now, quickly, before there's total catastrophe, or to control everything or you will be exposed as useless. Intuition, in contrast, inspires no such panic or drama. It encourages you to slow down, to look more closely, and to contemplate a situation mindfully.

Also, intuitive thoughts never have a quality of harsh self-judgment. The Goblin will say things like "You can't do this. You haven't got what it takes!" while the intuition, which is connected with the Divine stream of consciousness, will say, "You can't do this right now. It's not the right timing for you, and you can be patient as you ready yourself."

Intuition says, "Beware! This is dangerous territory. Slow down and observe, and listen to your inner allies, who offer wisdom and compassionate guidance." The Goblin yells, "Beware! You aren't good enough, smart enough, or competent enough!" and insists that you should find some powerful allies outside of you.

If that financial advisor seems shady, or that potential romantic partner appears to be a little too charming and slick, the Goblin says, "You worry too much. You should feel lucky to have this person in your life." Or worse, he admits they're not what you want them to be and tells you this is a great opportunity to use these people to *your* advantage (the Goblin loves to make you confuse his needs with your own). "You can change others; you can make them be how you want them to be! You will be a great healer, and they will be beholden to you and love you forever!" the Goblin says, beginning his fast-talking sales pitch. If you hesitate, he'll start with the hard sell.

The warnings and judgments of the Goblin can't be trusted, because he's the ultimate trickster. Listen to him and he'll end up driving your proverbial bus while you're sitting in the backseat looking out the window, wondering why you're in a territory of fear, anger, discord, or sorrow.

Your Goblin's Origins and Purpose

Every Goblin has a birthday. He was born the day you were wounded. As he sprang forth from your pain, he grabbed a bone from you and ran away with it. Maybe this bone was your innocence, or your ability to trust others. It might have been your confidence, sense of self-worth, or ability to speak your truth.

Whatever it was you lost or were about to claim on that day, think of it as a bone that is hidden on the Island of Broken Dreams. You won't be able to heal the wound created when that Goblin was born until you reclaim your bone and incorporate it into yourself. The Goblin will do his best to stop you, but Spirit will help you.

Although the Goblin may seem bad, he's really not. He's mostly afraid of not existing at all, becoming powerless and homeless again after having found a home in *you*. Unfortunately, he is confused by who "you" are. Because his birthday is the day when you were wounded, he is totally identified with that trauma. That's why he can't recognize your higher self, which isn't traumatized and has different priorities from that of the wounded ego. The Goblin's goals clash with yours. He'll find ingenious ways to drive you toward situations that reinforce the wound.

Mischievous though he is, the Goblin has only one true power: mimicry. He'll speak to you in a voice you may mistake as belonging to your inner knowing. Get to know his voice—its quality, catchphrases, and favorite sayings—and you'll start to recognize when he's awake, active, and trying to influence you. Name him, call him out, and you take away his power. This is the lesson of the fairy tale "Rumpelstiltskin."

In the story, a miller brags to the king that his daughter can spin straw into gold. To save her father from embarrassment, the girl doesn't deny the outrageous claim and instead agrees to go to the palace and prove his boast. Terrified of having her and her father's lie exposed, she sits down at the spinning wheel in a room full of straw and begins to cry.

This is when the Goblin in this fairy tale, Rumpelstiltskin, shows up. He discovers the maiden's plight and offers to spin the straw into gold for her—for a price. For three days, he keeps her secret and spins straw into gold for her, in exchange for a necklace, a ring, and finally, the promise that she will give him her firstborn son.

The king, none the wiser, stops challenging the miller's daughter and proposes marriage. A year later, baby in arms, the queen has forgotten all about her promise to the Goblin when he shows up at her door. He demands the baby—unless she can guess his name.

The significance of this key point in the story is that when we name a Goblin, he no longer has power over us. We recognize the origin of our wound, and this is the beginning of our healing. In the fairy tale, the poor girl runs through every name she's ever heard of while Rumpelstiltskin taunts her and rubs his hands in glee at the prospect of gaining his prize. Finally, she sneaks out into the enchanted forest at night and spots the Goblin triumphantly dancing while singing his name. The next day she is able to send him away because she speaks his name and thus causes him to lose his claim over her.

In the same way, we wrest our power and break the spell of victimhood when we speak the truth about our Goblin. We stop living a lie, hiding from the truth that brings us shame.

This tricky Goblin is born with the intent of protecting something, but once he is rendered homeless, he's left without purpose, so he keeps himself busy by hiding the things you're uncomfortable seeing. Rather than protect hidden treasure, which was his job when he was a gnome under the earth, he protects and reinforces the deformed and twisted, the thoughts such as *I'm not worthy of love, I should be ashamed of myself, I'll never have enough,* and *I can't speak my truth.* He twists your behaviors, too, causing you to lie or cheat in order to gain power.

Every Goblin is also a transportation expert. When you find yourself in a difficult landscape, wondering how you got there, it's because he whisked you away when you weren't looking. If you're lost or frightened in the Sticky Swamp, he'll insist that you must get everything on your agenda done—and perfectly, too—or something awful will happen. Then he'll reassure you that *he* will be your guide. He'll tell you that you don't need your Compass of Spirit and that time is running out . . . and hey, he knows a great shortcut to Easy Street.

The Goblin is very skilled at wearing you down so that you'll let him drive the bus, steer the ship, and take charge of your psyche. Banish a Goblin and he'll come back even stronger. The only way to "rid" yourself of him is to tame him, and to do that, you must first listen to him, because he can give you insight into your wound. Don't pay attention to what he says, however. Just ask him, "What is your name and birthday?"

Then ask him what bone he stole from you. Exposed for who he is—a trickster—he will hang his head and admit that yes, he took the bone. He'll tell you its name and confess that you can find it on the Island of Broken Dreams, a place you can travel to on your own, without his help. Every wound involves a loss of something vital. What did you lose at that painful point in your past?

Thank the Goblin for his help (even if you do feel the urge to throttle him) and point out to him that he looks like he could use a nap. By taming the Goblin with this dialogue, you actually lull him to sleep. Encourage him to lay his head down on the forest floor as you cover him with a blanket. Soon, he'll begin to snore, and then you can continue your journey unimpeded. In this way, your Goblin won't achieve his aim of getting you to identify with your wound. Instead, you will have tamed him and taken away his power—at least until he awakens again, which he will do when you get triggered by events that echo the past.

A Goblin Named Bulimia

We do extensive dialoguing with our Goblins in my weekend intensives in Sedona. Participants find out how to name their inner Goblins and learn how to locate a neutral place within themselves in order to observe what they've disowned. Writing exercises are crucial components of the work.

Here is a story about my bulimia, which I've long since overcome:

> One of my Goblins is named Bulimia, and he was born one day when I was 14 years old. I remember the exact moment this ugly creature started screaming inside me. I _felt_ rather than heard him shriek, but I imagine that the experience of "birthing" inside is the same as outside. The sense of being grotesque and out of control, in unbearable torment, reminds me of a real birth, when you're at the mercy of nature's agenda. This

delivery, though, was its dark opposite: I gave birth to this part of myself over a toilet bowl, vomiting its first bulimic breath.

I had just gotten my period and was confused about my newfound womanhood. I wanted to be free and express myself, but I was constantly getting the message that I should silence my wild self. I had vague memories of being violated at the age of six by our neighbor who babysat us, and that troubled me deeply. Boys started noticing me, but I was afraid of rejection because I was living in a constricting, regimented environment, and I feared they might see how imperfect I was. I believed that I was essentially dirty and unlovable, and I was full of shame.

I always felt as if I were boxed into some form that I didn't belong in. I tried hard to conform to people's expectations of me, but the more I tried, the more ungainly and flawed I felt. My feelings of inadequacy were my secret shame.

That day, the pressures had built up to the point that I snapped. I was taking a class at the German school my mother had forced me to attend so that I could learn her native language. Although I wished I could walk home with the other girls, my mother always insisted on driving me. She was very clear: she didn't want me to associate with anyone she didn't know. I hated going there, and just before class, I'd decided I needed relief in any form. I went to the candy store in the basement of the building and filled my satchel with cookies and chocolate bars. I'd never done that before with such determination.

I walked past the classroom and into the girls' restroom, sat in a stall, and ate every single thing I had, barely taking a breath. My heart was pounding so hard, and I was sweating. Then I knelt down and began to force myself to vomit. It was an act of defiance.

I repeated this behavior every time I was to go to class. Although I had savored this revenge against my mother the first time I did it, afterward I found I was powerless to stop myself. I really felt something "other" in charge. I had no idea that other girls were doing this, too, or that the behavior had a name: <u>bulimia.</u> I thought I was the only one who acted in this "shameful" way, which made me feel worse about myself.

Many women identify with this type of Goblin, as eating disorders such as anorexia, bulimia, or compulsive overeating have become more prevalent due to media pressure to look a certain way in order to be beautiful. It was years before I stopped mistreating my body through bingeing and purging and swallowing my anger, and by then I had given birth to new Goblins. I call them my "Goblin Village." I know I have a whole lot of them because I became a drug addict and an alcoholic.

Today I consider myself free because I've learned to love every single one of them . . . after all, they made me who I am today: sober now for years and healed from bulimia for a long time, too. Whenever I get triggered, I feel them stirring, and I just have to love them all for their twisted ways of trying to protect me.

Ancestral Goblins

Sometimes we don't even know a Goblin's birthday or name because it is an ancestral one handed down from our parents, grandparents, or great-grandparents.

I have a client, Alice, whose family lost everything in World War II, and whose mother was overprotective, always telling her to "be careful." Her mother had a stockpile of food in the basement "just in case" and hid money in socks that Alice would find when she would help with the laundry. Her mom constantly worried that "something might happen one day."

Alice could recall the palpable fear in her house, even though everyone was fine and there was no real threat. She grew into adulthood with an irrational fear of becoming a "bag lady." No matter how successful she became, she felt anxious and believed that everything would be lost.

Listening to this inherited voice had created real issues for her. Alice's choices reflected her fear that nothing would ever be enough to make her safe. When I suggested she look at this voice as a character separate from herself, an ancestral Goblin inherited from her mother, she was shocked to recognize how she'd allowed her financial anxieties to run her life and had cut herself off from being fully present to her joy.

We have to become aware of this scared little creature inside all of us and learn to be compassionate toward him. By creating this character and observing him, we can instantly disentangle ourselves from his hold on us and free ourselves to make choices from a higher place within. But to tame him quickly, we have to bypass the analytical part of the brain and enter into the creative realm. Only then can we avoid getting sucked into irrational fears about disaster that cause us to deny our problems.

What are your Goblins? What are their birth dates? When did they enter your world? The following exercise will help you find out.

Exercise: Discovering the Origins of Your Goblin

Just allow your imagination to flow as you create this unusual dialogue. If your Goblin begins acting out, insisting that there is nothing to be learned from this exercise, pay attention to him and be sure to write down what he says.

In your journal, rewrite the account of a painful incident in your past as the story of a Goblin's birth.

- Observe the Goblin that was born that day. What does he look like?

- How do you feel when you look into the eyes of your Goblin?

- What is he telling you about himself?

- If the Goblin you discover was born of a wound from your past, can you allow yourself to view him as innocent? Can you see him as the product of your fear and defensiveness?

- Can you allow yourself to feel compassion for him?

- What would it be like if caring for him and understanding him would allow you to be empowered?

The Chatterbox

The Chatterbox has a voice that is just as distracting as the Goblin's. The difference is that the Chatterbox won't take you to a place of self-judgment or hurt. He'll just talk your ear off and waste your time. Still, you have to learn to tame him so that you can move forward toward your goals and embrace the adventure of your life, rather than get stuck listening to his stream of non-sense.

You've heard the voice of the Chatterbox. His little lid flaps up and down as he narrates every moment of your busy day: "Oh, look, the phone's ringing. Caller ID, who is it? Telemarketer, don't answer—oops, forgot to turn the dishwasher on, let me get to that; yeah, the omelette was good this morning, need to pick up some more eggs . . . blah, blah, blah." Sometimes the Chatterbox has something of value to say: maybe you really do need to buy more eggs and turn on the dishwasher. But too often, the Chatterbox keeps your mind so busy sorting through its flood of thoughts that you can't attend to what's really important to you.

When was the last time you found yourself watching a tele-vision program only to suddenly realize you couldn't *possibly* care less about what the host was saying, and you just wasted ten min-utes listening to him? That chipper host is in your head, too, pre-venting you from listening to your inner wisdom.

The best way to shut down the Chatterbox or muffle his motor-mouth is to develop a meditation practice. If you're not good at sitting and meditating, make yoga or walking or some other activ-ity your meditation. The idea is to find a practice that slows the busy mind and awakens that part of you that observes without judgment: *Wow, my Chatterbox is really busy today. Let me just turn down the volume knob because I don't need to hear all this.* Work with a to-do list, and at least the "Gotta do this, gotta do that" part of his narrative will go away more quickly.

Exercise: Giving the Chatterbox Something to Do

Since the Chatterbox is the part of you that likes to talk incessantly, you can direct this voice intentionally to affirm the most positive words! Affirmations are powerful, and they work to train the Chatterbox to "chatter" about empowering things.

In your journal, write ten positive affirmations, and repeat them throughout the day for two weeks. You'll notice how quickly your Chatterbox will learn how to say them automatically. Here are my ten favorites:

1. I am living my *best* life now!

2. Everything I need comes to me easily and effortlessly.

3. God is the source of my supply, and that supply is endless.

4. I am only given what I can handle every day.

5. My life is getting better every day in every way!

6. What is mine will not go past me.

7. I am beautiful just as I am.

8. I am only attracted to food that is good for me.

9. Spirit leads me to my highest good, always.

10. The light within me creates miracles in my life now!

Don't forget to repeat these, or *your* ten favorites, as many times as you can throughout the day.

Pay close attention to your emotions when you hear the Chatterbox blathering on. If you're feeling bad about yourself, fearful, or depressed, it's probably because that sneaky Goblin has ventured into the Chatterbox; and when you look closely, under the lid are those beady eyes and the big mouth with garish teeth saying to you, "You didn't do what you were supposed to do, again? Boy, are you disorganized. No wonder your life is such a mess . . . blah, blah, blah."

Learning to differentiate between these two voices of your ego isn't difficult. Your thoughts may run something like this scenario:

Ah, cheesecake. I don't want to have too much, as it's too rich, but a little taste would be nice. Yes, that's lovely . . . my friend is talking now—she isn't happy; I wonder why not. Interesting what she's saying. This is the Chatterbox. The internal dialogue is benign, although constant.

The Goblin is the voice that jumps in and says, "Cheesecake?! You're eating cheesecake, you fat slob? You are so fat; and you're going to be fat, fat, fat! All you do is eat. No one loves you; look at your fat stomach. You're such a loser. You should eat that piece and then eat more so you don't have to listen to *her* anymore. That's right!" This is the Goblin, having crawled into the Chatterbox. You start feeling bad, disempowered, and you pull yourself out of the enjoyment of having a bite, into self-reproach and punishment. You end up focusing on the awful running monologue.

By becoming aware of the voices of the Goblin and Chatterbox, you empower yourself to quiet them. The Goblin has a hard time squeezing into the Chatterbox when positive directed statements are being repeated. That's when the most marvelous magic begins: when you become conscious that there are other voices, other enchanted creatures, who can help you on this adventure.

Exercise: Goblinspeak Retraining

In your journal, jot down a list of the things you repeat to yourself that are self-sabotaging or negative. Then beside each entry transform the statement into a positive affirmation. Every time you hear your Goblin use negative affirmations, slow down and turn it around. Here are some examples:

Goblinspeak: "I'm so fat. I'm disgusting."

Retrained: "I love and approve of myself whatever size I may be!"

Goblinspeak: "No one will ever love me—I'm damaged."

Retrained: "No matter what has happened to me in the past, I am lovable just as I am!"

Goblinspeak: "Why isn't he into me? What can I do to change myself to convince him?"

Retrained: "If this man doesn't love me, he's not the one for me. I now attract a partner who is right for me in every way."

Goblinspeak: "I'm going to be a bag lady. I'm never going to find a good job."

Retrained: "I attract the perfect job for me at the perfect time. It's wonderful that I've had the opportunity to take a little break from work. I always have what I need, no matter what."

Traveler's Notes

- You're distracted from your intuition by the voice of your ego.

- Your ego's voice can be helpful, benign, or troublesome. Very often, it's troublesome.

- It's helpful to imagine the ego's voice as a mythological creature you can interact with: a mischievous, trickster Goblin; or a benign, distracting Chatterbox.

- Goblins who are untamed will whisk you off to emotionally challenging landscapes.

- Untamed Goblins will also trick you into believing that your ego's needs are all-important.

- An untamed Goblin will steep you in fear.

- You can't shut off the voice of the ego, but you can reduce its influence on you.

- You quiet the ego by listening to it and having compassion for the parts of yourself that are difficult to accept.

- Every Goblin, which represents a wound to the ego, has a birthday and a name.

- You can inherit a Goblin from your parents, grandparents, or great-grandparents.

- When you identify a Goblin—that is, when you name him and discover his origin—you'll reduce his power over you.

- The Goblin stole a bone from you that you must reclaim on the Island of Broken Dreams. It is a quality you lost when you experienced a threat to yourself and became wounded.

- You quiet an overly busy Chatterbox by meditating and slowing down your thoughts so they don't dominate your consciousness.

- The Chatterbox can be trained to repeat positive affirmations that make it difficult for the Goblin to squeeze in and start talking.

⤳ Chapter Five ⤳

YOUR
MAGICAL ALLIES

---

*"That inner voice has both gentleness and clarity.
So to get to authenticity, you really keep going down to
the bone, to the honesty, and the inevitability of something."*

— MEREDITH MONK

"Wisdom begins in wonder."

— ATTRIBUTED TO SOCRATES

At any moment that you decide to be mindful and become aware, something fantastic happens: You start to recognize where you are, when you are, and whom you're listening to. You can awaken your inner Wizard of Awareness, who helps you tap into your intuition, your inner knowing, and the wisdom of the great consciousness that is available to everyone.

How do I have any idea what is really going on in some stranger's life when I do a reading? How can I tell you that six months from now you're going to be making a major move? It's because I'm sitting in that wizard's chair, accessing the incredible wisdom of the universe. Detached from my self, I reach out into the vastness of awareness and "see" the pathways as they form in their myriad magical ways.

As soon as you take out the Compass of Spirit, you summon this wizard from his sunny meditation chamber, a sanctuary of quiet where he can listen to your call and answer your need for guidance. The Wizard of Awareness doesn't speak, because he's an observer. But don't let his silence fool you. His powers are extraordinary. Follow him to his enchanted chair, placed at a high point above the landscape, and notice that as he sits down, he is beckoning you. You can actually be seated exactly where he is, for he is ethereal and part of you.

As you settle into this chair, you pick up his magic wand and notice that your name is on it. You stretch your arm forward, and the light at the wand's tip illuminates a stream of air that was hidden until now. You sense that this stream is an inexhaustible supply of wisdom that is always there if you know how to find it. Sitting in this chair gives you an objective perspective because you're no longer immersed in your emotions or beliefs. Your vista is much larger, your view much clearer. Possibilities you hadn't thought of or imagined begin to reveal themselves when you're in the wizard's chair.

You dip your wand into the stream, and then you begin to hear the whispers. Your intuition, and the Great Unconscious, is speaking to you through your allies. Cast your eyes about and you'll start to see them appear.

Now if you choose not to summon the Wizard of Awareness because you're mesmerized by the incessant narration of the Chatterbox or the trash-talking of the Goblin, the kindly old wizard will become impatient and kick you in the seat of the pants or bop you over the head with his wand. Suddenly awake to the call from your intuition, you have two choices: you can become quiet and discover the wisdom that will assist you on this leg of the journey; or you can resist, and continue to blunder through your landscape and unconsciously react to the events around you . . . as you wonder why your head and your rear end are sore.

Sit in the chair of the Wizard of Awareness and you'll find that hidden allies begin to appear in this landscape: the Gentle Gardener and the Spirit of Place. You'll also have a chance to meet the twin sister of the Gentle Gardener, the Bone Collector, who lives on the Island of Broken Dreams and can restore you to wholeness and well-being. Quiet the Goblin and Chatterbox now and get ready to meet these extraordinary creatures who inhabit your Map.

Be still and become aware of these allies within you, the voices of your intuition, who have access to great wisdom. No matter how traumatizing the landscape, these guiding characters are there for you. They patiently await your readiness to receive their wisdom and are prepared to act immediately as soon as they're called into your consciousness. If you're too mesmerized by the voice of the Goblin to remember your compass or take a seat in the chair, the wizard will ensure that you remember what you're supposed to do—and the allies will call out to you. They're concerned with your well-being and are always looking out for your best interests.

However, sometimes these allies can seem like challengers. They know that to lift you out of your grief or misery, they must shine the harsh light of truth upon your life. Trust them, for they won't hurt you unless they absolutely must for the sake of your growth.

Remember, you're never trapped. Retrieve your Compass of Spirit and claim your ability to interact with your Map.

The Twin Sisters

While the Goblin is the representation of the shadow self, the twin sisters—the Bone Collector and the Gentle Gardener— personify the light: They are light bearers who allow you to see into the dark corners. Each carries a lantern underneath her cloak to illuminate the terrain. The Bone Collector uses it to find what you thought was lost, while the Gentle Gardener uses it to help you see the land, pointing out which soil is the most fertile for planting the seeds of your intention, and reminding you of what you've sown. Are you ready to see what they have come to show you?

Imagine these sisters as timeless beings, embodiments of primal wisdom that have always been present, even before you took your human form. Together, they personify the knowing, eternal part of the self that is always there, but which you may overlook until you undergo tribulations and embrace radical transformation so that you can give birth to a new *you*.

The Bone Collector

The Bone Collector is an old woman who lives on the Island of Broken Dreams, a place accessible from the Valley of Loss and the Vandalized House. When you've been violated and are in the Vandalized House, feeling vulnerable and hurt, it appears that someone took your power, but that's not actually the case. In fact, your violator has merely rendered your power invisible, and you have unwittingly conspired in this illusion. The Bone Collector knows this.

Whenever you're betrayed, mistreated, or taken advantage of, you lose something of value. It may be your innocence or your ability to trust. It may be your dignity and sense of self-worth.

After I was raped, I couldn't bear to think about the bad choices I'd made in my inebriated state: I had ignored my friends' warnings about a bar and the men who congregated there because I had such a powerful need to see myself as daring and rebellious. After accepting a ride home from three men who took advantage of the situation, not only was I too terrified to fight back, but afterward, I didn't report the assault. To avoid my feelings of shame and guilt, I eroticized the experience, then connected myself to these men later on. The trauma bonded me to them, as I couldn't accept that

I had been so violated. I began to act from the deep, dark belief that I was damaged goods. I re-traumatized myself again and again by making more bad choices about dangerous men, drinking, and dicey situations.

If only I'd known to visit the land of the Bone Collector, who would accept me and care for me. I had no idea that deep within me were the bones I had lost, all carefully guarded by this kind soul who would make sure they were there for me when I was ready to reclaim them. I had to love and forgive the girl whose need for the illusion of invulnerability caused her to walk into a dangerous situation and keep returning to that place in one form or another.

The Bone Collector, who tends to all that we fear is lost, is an aspect of Mother Earth. Like *La Loba* and other creatures in indigenous myths retold by Clarissa Pinkola Estés in *Women Who Run with the Wolves,* the Bone Collector is the aspect of nature that ensures that nothing is ever truly lost. Nature is the great recycler, finding a use for everything. What we lost may change form, but it is always there. As Estés writes:

> In archetypal symbology, bones represent the indestructible force. They do not lend themselves to easy reduction. They are by their structure hard to burn, nearly impossible to pulverize. In myth and story they represent the indestructible soul-spirit. We know the soul-spirit can be injured, even maimed, but it is very nearly impossible to kill.
>
> You can dent the soul and bend it. You can hurt it and scar it. You can leave the marks of illness upon it, and the scorch marks of fear. But it does not die, for it is protected by *La Loba* in the underworld. She is both the finder and the incubator of the bones.

The Bone Collector has a sacred junkyard where there is no junk, only what she has salvaged and what she knows has value. Others see only bones, dead and brittle. She sees their potential and can breathe life back into them. She does this by holding the bone to her lips and singing a magical song. Then she hands the revivified bone to you so that you can bring it back into your body. It will strengthen your skeleton and your spine, the structures that keep you together and moving forward on this adventure.

Whenever you doubt your strength, remember that whatever the bone you may have lost or perhaps never claimed, you can find it on the Island of Broken Dreams, where it was left by the Goblin who was born from your pain. You can ask the Bone Collector to return it to you. Gladly, she will sing it back to life and celebrate its return with you. You have to ask, though, as she springs to life only when you're willing to face the truth about the past. With the bone reincorporated into yourself, you become whole again.

The Gentle Gardener

The Bone Collector's twin sister is the Gentle Gardener. She, too, is an aspect of Mother Earth. She expresses love and cares about all that matters to you. With her green thumb, she can make anything grow because she infuses it all with life force.

What is it that you want her to give life to? Is it your anger, or your dreams? Take care what you plant. The Gentle Gardener makes no judgments, however, so she will apply her skill to anything you choose to plant—whether it's an apple tree, a fragrant rosebush, or thistles and weeds—and ensure that it grows. She will make no distinction about what to nurture unless you ask her to, for all seeds are precious to her, even the ones that yield poisonous fruit. She knows that everything that grows in the garden can have value that isn't apparent upon first glance.

The Gentle Gardener is helped by the garden gnomes who live under the earth and watch over what is still a seed in the stage of potential. The Gentle Gardener knows exactly where each one is planted, which soil is rocky, and which is deeply fertile. She knows how to work with any terrain to make your flowers grow.

In the harvest land, the Gentle Gardener makes sure the leaves are turning the right colors; and in the summer meadow, she is in charge of the sun and the rain. She knows when the carpet of violets will reveal itself at the base of the Maple tree, and sends the gentle breezes that spread the wispy seedpods of the dandelions. The Gentle Gardener personifies patience and acceptance because she knows that what is dormant will come back to life, and what is vital and supple will someday become dead and brittle and then break down into nourishment for the soil.

Like her sister, the Bone Collector, the Gentle Gardener lets nothing go to waste. In any landscape, from the Frozen Land to the Storm Fields, she can find something to use in her garden. She will always be able to locate places for you to plant seeds because she knows that grass can sprout from a crack in cement, and life can flourish in the crevices of a dead tree lying on the forest floor.

The Gentle Gardener will caution you to take care where you tread because underneath the earth there are things still un-formed. She knows the potential of any landscape, and knows that what you have planted must be nourished and protected.

You can confide in her about your secret desire to make money by following your passion, and she'll smile knowingly and point to a tiny seedling you had overlooked. She'll tell you that she has been caring for it while you've wandered from place to place, look-ing for the support that was here all along.

She knows how to help you grow your ability to express your-self through dance and movement, as you let go of your relation-ship to your body as something that has been damaged or has betrayed you. She reminds you that she's able to do this because she has a sister who has been guarding that lost part of you that loved your skin, your belly, and your corporeal form, which is in-tegral to who you are.

The Gentle Gardener's wisdom is boundless, and she is happy to explain the rhythm of the seasons and teach you how to feel them in your blood and your bones so that you don't rush or resist change. Look for her when you're lost or worried, feeling pres-sured, or stuck in procrastination. She'll listen to all you have to say and share her insights with you. Don't ask her to change the elements of the landscape, though, for she's the one who ensures its integrity. She knows that a desert needs heat and spiny cacti;

and that a jungle needs humidity and a dense, green canopy. She'll help you find peace and wisdom in this land, but she won't collude with you in your denial of it.

The Gentle Gardener and the Field of Dreams

The Field of Dreams is actually a magical garden, a living system where the seeds of your thoughts, feelings, and beliefs germinate. Life grows here above ground, where we can see it; and beneath the surface, where it is unseen and connected through complex root systems.

Your thoughts and desires are like seeds scattered across the soil and either left to grow wild or tended to by an unseen hand. The Gentle Gardener can teach you how to nurture the fragile shoots and care for the earth, and she'll exhort you not to sit idly waiting for your plants to grow. Listen to her and you'll avoid the Ghostlands of nostalgia and wishful thinking.

The Gentle Gardener can identify which is a weed; and which is a flowering plant, herb, or vegetable stalk. If you want to know about the relationship you've just begun or a situation you've just entered into, ask her about its nature and qualities. If you want to nurture the seeds of intention, ask her what you must do. She'll take out her lantern from beneath her cloak and shine a light on those seedlings. Are you prepared to do the work you need to do? Are you willing to accept the parameters of your map?

If you plant a seed, its growth will be determined by the conditions of the environment, as well as your attention to its welfare. There's an invisible energy exchange that's always moving "behind the scenes" to support the life path of the seed. The ideas you have about who you are in the world (and where you think you're supposed to be going) are similar. The harvest occurs when the plants in the field mature and are ready to bear fruit. You can't hasten the seasons of growth by force or by wanting everything according to your wishes. You plant the seed and move on to other things, allowing life to have its wonderful mysterious way in its own time. Much is going on behind the scenes, under the ground.

My father used to say that if I water the seed of every thought—every dream I plant in the ground of my life—often enough, it will develop into strong, rooted acts and ideas. He said those seeds encapsulate the pure potential of energy that would then grow and thrive, strengthened by an accompanying belief, until it was visible in my outer life.

"You will reap what you sow" is a biblical saying rich with wisdom. Our subconscious minds store many seeds, and we unwittingly plant them along with the ones of our conscious choices. We sometimes end up with weeds because the seeds we plant consciously aren't strong enough—and sometimes, our *map* determines what will be able to grow in our Field of Dreams.

The Spirit of Place

The ancient Romans believed in magical beings called *genius loci,* the Spirits of Place. Sprites, nymphs, brownies, fairies, and leprechauns are all examples of the ways in which people have personified the spiritual landscape of a given natural locale. While in myth these creatures may be tricksters—you might be surprised by how nasty those pretty little fairies can be in the old European folktales—in the Map, they leave the mischief to the Goblins. They wait in silence for you to contact the Wizard of Awareness. Sit in his chair and they'll suddenly appear.

Each Spirit of Place is a tour guide to the land where he or she dwells, telling you every feature, from the slope of the hills to the number of leaves on the trees. The Spirit of Place knows that this land, like any other, has both shadow and light. He or she can reveal to you the wisdom of the place and the magical tools hidden there that you can use to see all that it has to offer—and that you can use to escape when it's time.

Let's meet some of these magical allies. . . .

— **The Ice Fairy.** This beautiful princess, with her piercing, crystal eyes, dwells in the Frozen Land. She will cover you with a magical white cape that will keep you warm even as you put on ice that which has been angering and frustrating you. She'll teach you patience and the ability to let go of what needs to die. The Ice Fairy will also inspire you with the hope of the winter solstice and the gradual rebirth of the sun, which brings longer days, conducive to planting. She'll tell you that if you're here in the Frozen Land, it's because you need to quietly plan what is next, as you let go of what must no longer be.

— **The Man in the Immovable Mountain.** Much as you might want to blast through the obstacle of the Immovable Mountain, you may not have enough dynamite to do so. Become quiet and ask the Man in the Mountain why you're here. Are you meant to learn other ways to deal with challenges? Are you meant to recognize *your* role in planting mountains in the middle of your path? The Man in the Mountain has many wonderful secrets for getting around this great barrier. He'll point the way to a winding path that will take you to the other side, or provide you with magic wings that allow you to become a bird and fly over his peak. He also knows a thing or two about mastery, perseverance, and the pride in having worked hard to achieve a goal.

— **The Ogre in the Sticky Swamp.** This fellow looks fierce but is actually a kind and gentle creature. Like the fictional ogre Shrek, he can show you the delights of mud and muck, bugs and beetles. This Spirit of Place will wait for you when you feel crazed with far too much to do and you become so overwhelmed with so many ideas that your head spins. He prevents you from drowning and holds you up when you get attached to that feeling of being preoccupied and distracted. He knows the value of slowing down and taking things one at a time—and the dark side of falling in love with your self-importance as a "very busy person." He'll also warn you about letting distractions trap you here.

— **The Woodland Sprite.** The Woodland Sprite knows where the grove you seek is and how easy it is to not see the forest for the trees . . . or the trees for the forest . . . because she understands perspective. She knows each leaf and twig, and the patterns of this complex environment. She'll help you see that when the way is dark, you may be on the verge of an opening. She'll remind you to look where you're walking, yet gaze up at the sky as well, where the constellations will remind you of where you are and your connection to Spirit.

— **The Faerie of the Raging River.** The Raging River can sweep you up in its current, sending you on a terrifyingly wild ride downstream. If this should happen, call upon the Faerie of the Raging River. She'll ensure that there is a branch you can grab on to, but you have to be willing to accept that the river has sent you to another spot on its bank. She can tell you how to get to the place along the river where you want to be. She'll also teach you the valuable lesson of going with the flow and accepting that you can't always build a bridge between yourself and someone you love.

— **The Thundering Spirit of the Storm Fields.** His voice is loud, but it's hard to make out what he's saying unless you let go of your fear, stop, and listen carefully. This Spirit will help you find shelter and show you why sometimes you need to be in this stormy land. He'll underscore your role in creating those lightning bolts that so frighten you, and guide you in using your anger more productively: to spark new ideas, momentum, and impetus. He knows that all storms clear the air and send the seeds of the trees caught up in the blustery wind to faraway places, where they can generate new growth and forests. He also knows that the rain nourishes the parched, barren land. Likewise, the lightning destroys faulty foundations, taking down the dead tree so that it can serve life in a new way, becoming a haven for insects and tiny creatures.

— **The Brownie at the Resting Tree.** Busy, busy, busy—as an adventurer on the Map, you need a break sometimes. The Brownie at the Resting Tree can teach you the value of slowing down and becoming still. She'll show you that the world will get along just fine if you take a break, and the brownies will attend to some of those tasks you were certain no one else could possibly address. The world will continue spinning if you sit down to rest. Here, you do without doing and everything gets done!

— **The Nymph of the Tranquil Lake.** The Nymph of the Tranquil Lake will teach you the value of reflection, and how to look deeply into yourself. She will caution you about becoming like Narcissus, who, according to Greek mythology, fell in love with his own reflection in the still waters. The Nymph will encourage you to gaze at yourself with compassion so that you may see yourself as you really are and experience acceptance and peace.

— **The Ruthless Balancer.** This Spirit's realm is the Land of Unfairness. When you're in survival mode, the Ruthless Balancer teaches you to throw away bones like vulnerability and softness. He explains that you need to lose some bones in order to be flexible. If you complain that life is unfair, he'll tell you that nature has a balance well beyond human comprehension, and you have to live with this truth. He can even show you a virus that is found in the Amazon that only destroys one species of ant, which is responsible for pollinating one particular flower. The virus keeps a perfect balance between ants, flowers, and the ecosystem. To the affected ant, contracting the virus is a terrible affliction, but from a larger perspective, it's necessary and part of the fabric of the rain forest.

We, too, must learn to understand that when life appears to be ruthless, it may be that we have to undergo something to achieve balance in our lives and in our world.

Cooperation, balance, unity, and flux require that animals destroy other animals in the cycle of life. The Ruthless Balancer knows that the Native Americans thanked the spirit of the bison they killed, showing gratitude for its sacrifice and respect for nature's equilibrium.

When we become too ruthless ourselves, we upset the scales. When *we* are the victims of ruthlessness, we must create our own balance, and the Ruthless Balancer can teach us how to do so. We must take life on life's terms and trust this Spirit.

He also knows that like Job in the Bible, you can lose everything and gain even more, but you have to be willing to let go of what you have. You may have to trade in your health temporarily to regain spiritual strength, or relinquish a marriage to find your voice.

The Ruthless Balancer brings order to chaos and gives meaning to suffering. He inspires you to have faith in a larger order.

These are just a few of the Spirits of Place; you'll surely meet others on your journey. Your soul will inspire your imagination to discover your own cast of magical characters within you. These enchanted beings created in your own mind can tell you about your relationship to their landscape, and how you might move through it differently and more quickly, staying only as long as needed.

First, however, you must discover who they are, because recognizing them will help you understand the lesson of your emotional experience, which forms a particular landscape. The following exercise will allow you to *observe*. In the next chapter, you'll take a more active role in the landscape and actually converse with those you find in the hills, woods, and rivers within you.

Exercise: Discover Your Inner Landscape and Its Inhabitants

Use the In-Vizion process (introduced in Chapter 2) to discover your current emotional landscape by letting your subconscious mind reveal it to you through imagery. Do this by focusing on your breath, and breathing slowly and deeply until you feel relaxed and your busy mind has quieted down. Let a landscape that represents your inner emotions arise in your mind's eye. Let your senses take in its sights, smells, and sounds.

Ask yourself:

- "What is this place?"

- "What do I see here?"

- "What am I doing here? How am I interacting with this land—hanging, swimming, climbing, or something else?"

- "When am I in time? Have I been here before?
  Do I know why I'm here and what I need to do?"

- "Do I know how to escape? Am I ready to leave, or
  ready to learn? Which do I need to be?"

Observe what is happening around you. Now look more closely. Are there any imaginary beings you can see moving about the land? Notice who they are and what they're doing. Later you'll dialogue with them, but for now, just watch quietly. Your inner wisdom will animate them, just as it fills in the details of the terrain and your relationship to it.

When you've finished observing this land and the beings here, describe it all in your journal.

In the next chapter, you'll dialogue with a Spirit of Place, the Gentle Gardener, or the Bone Collector. You'll find that these conversations can transform you, just as an honest exchange with that tricky little Goblin can. Whatever setting you find yourself in, if you can describe it and imagine it, the Spirit of Place will arrive with a message for you. It is revealed when you understand the nature of the place's attributes. Then the Spirit becomes a sacred oracle for you, always ready to assist!

Traveler's Notes

- It's helpful to imagine enchanted allies who dwell in the Map and can assist you.

- The magical allies are figments of your imagination and aspects of your own psyche, so they're always accessible to you and will always answer your questions and help you.

- Allies can sometimes seem like challengers because they shed the harsh light of truth on your life, but they exist to guide you and share with you the wisdom that is currently hidden from your conscious mind.

- If you imagine that your mindful self is a Wizard of Awareness, you can take his seat at any time, raise his wand, and tap into your own unconscious, as well as the Divine river of awareness itself.

- There are twin sisters who personify your inner knowing: the Bone Collector, who lovingly collects and watches over any quality you've left unclaimed or lost as a result of an emotional wounding; and the Gentle Gardener, who tends any thoughts, feelings, or beliefs you "plant" in your mind.

- Only ask, and the Bone Collector will breathe life back into what you have lost and return it to you.

- It's up to you to let the Gentle Gardener know which "plants" you'd prefer not to grow and to choose the elements of your life's garden wisely, for she tends to all that has been planted.

- Each inner emotional landscape holds great lessons that you can learn with the help of a Spirit of Place, a part of your psyche that recognizes what you need to understand and accept.

- A Spirit of Place is an imaginary, enchanted ally who serves as an oracle, arriving anytime you identify your emotions as an inner landscape and describe its features. Observing this landscape, you may begin to discover its wisdom.

~ *Chapter Six* ~

CONVERSATIONS AND MAGICAL TRANSFORMATIONS

"Fear is a question: What are you afraid of, and why? Just as the seed of health is in illness, because illness contains information, our fears are a treasurehouse of self-knowledge if we explore them."

— MARILYN FERGUSON

"As the sun on rising makes the world active, so does self-awareness effect changes in the mind. In the light of calm and steady self-awareness, inner energies wake up and work miracles without any effort on your part."

— SRI NISARGADATTA MAHARAJ

Do you feel alone in your struggles? You aren't, you know. On your Map, there are archetypal, fictional characters that represent aspects of your psyche. These magical allies and challengers can be used to access the wisdom within that's hidden from your conscious mind, which thinks too much and blocks your intuition.

Some of this wisdom you've acquired through your life experiences, but some comes to you from a higher source: Spirit, who bestows the gift of insight when you feel that you're flying blind. Whispering to you through your intuition, Spirit is eager to dialogue with you. The device of interacting with magical allies on your Map facilitates these exchanges with Spirit and your subconscious. This helps you break out of the limitations that your logical mind creates; and the illusions that your trickster Goblin, or wounded ego, conjures up.

Spirit knows we are not our behavior; that we are ever changing; that there is always potential for growth, new possibilities, and great transformation. Using the Map, we can more easily remember that we can walk away from the distressing landscapes of our past and step into a more wholesome terrain. We do this more readily when we enter into dialogue with our magical allies and challengers.

You can emotionally experience the return of any quality you feel that you lost as a result of the events in your life. When you lack faith in your ability to heal yourself, to change your beliefs and self-talk, or to break old destructive habits, turn to Spirit. Take out the compass that points to true north and let the enchanted beings of your psyche come into your imagination, where you can fancy that they're talking to you, guiding you, and helping you transform.

These dialogues may be very emotionally intense, because hidden from your conscious mind are often the truths that you find most painful. By dialoguing with imaginary aspects of your psyche, you may find it easier to accept what you have to learn about yourself and your life than if you were just to use your logical mind to figure out "what's wrong."

Your magical allies can show you the shadow and light of any quality and any situation, and help you embrace possibilities. Dialogues with them will open your mind so that you feel expansive and hopeful instead of contracted, forlorn, and trapped in your emotional experiences and the limitations you perceive. These creatures will connect you to the magic of Spirit, who can perform the impossible and brings light to all the darkest corners.

Learning Goblinspeak

The first ally to dialogue with is that trickster Goblin, who will not quiet down until you hear what he has to tell you. Irritating though his voice may be, remember that it is worth listening to, because he always knows the origin of your wounds.

When the Goblin is speaking, you must first become aware that it is *his* voice, not yours, that is guiding you. Then you have to tune out all his misleading information to get to the heart of what he really wants to tell you. When you do, he'll be deeply relieved, because you've listened and truly heard what he has to say. *You* will be relieved, too, because you'll have insight into your feelings, beliefs, and actions.

To get beyond his babbling, you have to learn to interpret Goblinspeak. He *is* speaking your language, but he talks very quickly, like a good con artist does. Sit in the wizard's chair and you'll magically slow down the Goblin's gibberish. Then you can carefully listen to what he's saying and discern what his message is.

The following two exercises, "A Portrait of Your Goblin" and "A Dialogue with Your Goblin," will help you uncover the wisdom that lies hidden in the shadows of your subconscious. Working with the archetype of the Goblin will allow you to do so in an emotionally safe way.

I suggest you perform the first exercise, which involves journaling, and then do the more challenging second one, which is a guided visualization. You might also incorporate a simple conversation with the Goblin into the guided visualization using the questions in the first exercise, which is what I do in my workshops. If you get stumped while journaling, use visualization to open the door to the thoughts and emotions that are painful to access, and let the imaginary Goblin speak to you.

Exercise: A Portrait of Your Goblin

Take out your journal so that you can record your answers to the questions in this exercise (alternatively, you can confront your Goblin and ask him these questions as part of the visualization that follows, then write out the responses afterward).

First, imagine that within you is a mischievous little creature who is responsible for all your negative self-talk, your habits that you feel ashamed of, and your beliefs about yourself that cause you to experience low self-worth. Think of him as an ugly, small beast who can't hurt you unless you follow his terrible advice and hurt *yourself.* You are in control of the Goblin, although he will never admit it. Take a deep breath and face this mythical aspect of yourself.

- What is your Goblin's name?

- When was he born?

- What does your Goblin have to say to you?

- Is what he says true for you, or is it a belief designed solely to keep him busy and feeling important?

The day he was born, the Goblin stole one of your bones, an important part of yourself that you need for healing. What has he stolen from you? What do you need to claim or reclaim?

Can you give the Goblin what he wants, and express love and compassion toward him? If not, can you transform him into a creature you can cuddle, love, and reassure?

If your Goblin appears too scary or repulsive, you might consider choosing a less frightening image—say, a troll doll or a character from a film, such as the "Mogwai" in the movie *Gremlins*. As part of this exercise, you may wish to draw a picture of your Goblin. What does he look like?

Exercise: A Dialogue with Your Goblin

Sit quietly, in a place where you know you'll be undisturbed, at a time when you're ready to let go of the constraints of your agenda, and take the time you need to learn what your Goblin has to tell you.

Breathe deeply, in and out, just noticing your breath and what it feels like to inhale slowly and exhale slowly. You might think In as you inhale and Out as you exhale to remain focused on the present moment, the present experience. Notice the thoughts and sensations that arise, but don't give them any weight. They are ephemeral, part of the wind. Let them pass before you. Don't let them move you. They will fade as they float off into the distance, away from your focus.

In this state of observation and nonjudgment, just listen to your Goblin. You're about to separate out the wheat from the chaff, as they say—the wisdom from the nonsense.

Notice that the Goblin's speech has slowed considerably. See his words before you, as if projected onto a screen. Observe their quality. Is this a thought with the emotion of fear, or sadness? What are you feeling?

Watch your feelings and thoughts rise, then fall; glow with intensity, then fade.

Notice that a certain thought is very strong. It doesn't fade—or it does, but comes back again and again. What is this thought? Ask yourself, Is this true for me?

Is it? Or is it the detritus of old conditioning, discarded ideas that are cluttering your thought processes like dirt gunking up your gears? Is this a thought to banish to the Canyon of Echoes, where it can reverberate against the walls harmlessly until it fades, no longer held captive in your heart, your mind, your body? Wave it away with a sweep of your wand. Watch it dim and fade as it is carried on the wind to the Canyon of Echoes, far away.

If the thought or belief is true for you, let yourself feel the pain of your emotions. Notice the experience of crying, sobbing, feeling anger rise within you.

The Goblin has given you a precious gem of an insight. You are able to appreciate that even as you watch him stomp his feet while steam comes out of his ears.

You smile indulgently, because the Goblin never understands that you are not him. He thinks he is protecting you, but really he is just pressuring you into identifying with your wounded self, and you've already made the decision not to do that. You are not him. You are not your wounds.

You know you have work to do, further healing to attend to. Tell the Goblin his name and his birth date. Let this knowledge come to you. As you speak it out loud, his shoulders drop.

"You are right—that's who I am," he says. Now you have power over him, because you know his name and origin. He sighs.

Thank the Goblin for his message. Notice how his rapid, shallow breathing begins to slow and deepen. He is becoming calm. His gnarly little fingers unclench. His eyelids begin to droop. You ask him to lie down in the soft grass near the roots of your tree, then give him a kiss on his forehead and lay a baby's blanket over him. Wait for a moment . . . he's beginning to snore.

Sit in silence, wand in hand. Recognize your power to tap into Source. No matter how harsh the landscape, you retain this power and you will use it. You're going to be okay. You <u>are</u> okay.

A Conversation with the Bone Collector

The Bone Collector and Gentle Gardener, sisters who serve as your enchanted allies, can help you reclaim your bone and begin to create something new for yourself. To summon them, just take your place in the chair of the Wizard of Awareness. They will appear, and let you know what you need to do.

The Bone Collector knows what you've lost or misplaced, because she has it for you on her Island of Broken Dreams. Your negative beliefs about yourself make it difficult for you to get to that enchanted land. Self-loathing, shame, a sense that "I don't deserve to reclaim that bone," or a belief that you're not good enough to have within you the qualities you desire all keep you from the island. Silence the Goblin and summon the Bone Collector . . . and she'll show you that you can trust again. You can get your dignity back, or the wonder you had as a child.

One of my clients, Charlotte, was on the brink of womanhood at age 15 when she found out that her father had had a string of mistresses and, exposed at last, he decided to leave her and her mother. Charlotte lost a bone that day—the bone of trust in men—and for many years, she found herself in relationships with partners who betrayed her.

She also never assimilated a "bone" she was on the verge of claiming: the belief that she was worthy of being treated with respect and loyalty by a man she loved. Seeing how her mother had tried so hard to be a good wife yet had been cast aside by her husband, Charlotte couldn't bring herself to believe that she could claim that bone of worthiness. Although she declared that she'd never end up like her mother, in the unseen recesses of her mind's garden, another message had been planted. Deep down, Charlotte felt that worthiness was a "bone" reserved for other women, not her.

She needed to reclaim those bones in a way that made her comfortable: to retain the valuable lessons she had learned about trust, but be open to taking risks in relationships . . . to feel good about herself as a woman who had made mistakes and not see herself as damaged goods.

It's the Goblin who convinces you that you can't have what you need and desire. The Bone Collector knows better. She will bring you this forgotten bone and gladly sing it to life for you, or grind it into fertilizer you can use to foster the growth of a new dream.

Imagine for a moment that the Bone Collector has a bone for you that you want back, in its original form. It seems dried up and lifeless, but she can transform it by infusing it with Spirit. What are the words to her life-affirming song? Sing it with her!

Exercise: Listening to the Song of the Bone Collector

If you're ready to reclaim a bone in yourself, take out your journal and write the words of the Bone Collector's song. Which verses dance in your ears as you listen to her plaintive voice? If you feel moved to do so, turn on a recording device and sing her song aloud. What vitalizing, rejuvenating words come to you?

Take the words into your heart and believe them.

If the lyrics to the Bone Collector's song don't come to you easily, be gentle with yourself. Trust that they are there even if you can't make them out right now. You might come back and try this exercise again until you hear them.

When you do hear the words, open your heart. Don't resist their truth. Allow these words to become familiar to you. Like a teenager getting used to her developing body, or a middle-aged woman accepting the internal shifts that etch themselves on her face and her waistline, you'll need time to accept the changes you're experiencing. New beliefs about yourself won't take hold immediately. Allow the bone you've reclaimed to settle into you. Become one with it. Own it.

As Charlotte came to realize, sometimes we don't *want* to re-incorporate a bone into ourselves. In this case, we need only to transform it, with the Bone Collector's help.

Exercise: Transforming a Lost Bone, with Help from the Bone Collector

You can use this visualization to reclaim a quality, even if you'd like to alter that quality somewhat so that it will fit in with who you are today (for instance, reclaiming "the ability to trust, tempered by caution," instead of "lost innocence"). Meditate for a few minutes in a quiet place before you enter the magical realm of the Map and imagine this encounter and dialogue with the Bone Collector. Afterward, describe your experience in your journal.

You have found it on the Island of Broken Dreams: a lost bone, a quality that did not seem to be a part of you all these years, ever since the day you were wounded and it was stolen from you. Although you want to rejoice, your heart sinks, for you see that this bone is gray, brittle, and lifeless. Allow yourself to feel sad at how neglected this bone has been.

You feel the Bone Collector express her compassion toward you. You sense her unconditional love as you survey the bones before you.

As you look around this land, you remember an important lesson that nature teaches: What looks dead may simply be resting. In winter, the black branches of the trees, the shriveled vines, the dried-up bushes . . . all hold vitality within them. The Bone Collector is part of nature. She is able to sing life back into an old bone, just as spring breathes new life into the old.

Her kindness soothes you, and yet you hesitate. "Bone Collector, your offer is generous," you say, "but I'm not sure I want to reclaim this bone. I don't want to lose any of the wisdom I have gained, any of the new qualities I have claimed for myself. How can I incorporate this bone into myself so that it will support me and give me strength?"

With clarity and wisdom, the Bone Collector tells you the answer. You nod, for you realize that she is right. You can reclaim this bone in a different form, one that fits who you are today.

The Bone Collector leads you to a fire that crackles and sends sparks toward the stars as the night envelops them. She carefully places the bone into the fire, where it glows red, then blue, then green, before turning black and crumbling into ash. The fire settles into embers, then cools as the sun begins to rise over the sea. You watch patiently as you begin to imagine what your life will be like when you have reclaimed this quality in a form that works for you. You plan what you will plant in the Field of Dreams.

The Bone Collector opens a velvet pouch and begins to fill it with the sacred ashes. When she is done, she pulls its golden drawstring and hands it to you. You are to sprinkle these ashes in your Field of Dreams, where they will nourish whatever you choose to grow. Hold the bag to your heart. Feel its power.

You now find yourself in your Field of Dreams. You are ready to plant. What will you grow? How will this bone help you fertilize the seeds of your dreams?

A Lesson on Gardening from the Gentle Gardener

By now, you know how the Gentle Gardener works with her sister, the Bone Collector. She helps you plant seeds in the Field of Dreams, and shows you how to scatter the ashes of bones upon the ground to transform "what was" into "what shall be" as you nourish the soil that will support your dreams.

The Gentle Gardener will also show you what you planted. Don't curse the ground in your Field of Dreams if it has an unsatisfying, meager yield. It may seem that nothing is growing and you're in a Barren Desert. However, the Gentle Gardener is always tending this garden and has wise advice: Know what you're planting. Choose rich soil and take the time to prepare it. Don't scatter the seeds of weeds that will block out the sun as they start to grow. Don't force the Gentle Gardener to waste your resources watering wild vegetation while your prosperity plant struggles in parched soil, desperate to capture the sun that squeezes through the cracks between the humongous leaves of the towering stinkweeds.

The Gentle Gardener does her best with what you've given her. It's your job to do a better job of planning and planting.

As you get to work trimming the leaves and pruning the trees, letting go of relationships that aren't working and situations that are too trying and not producing enough of value for you, be proud of yourself for rolling up your sleeves and getting into the dirt. This is soul work, and you should give yourself credit for having the courage to make changes. But take a closer look at the weeds you're about to rip up by the roots.

Not every situation in life is what you'd like it to be, and your relationships can doubtless be very challenging. Yet there's something to be learned in every one of them. You may not want to cut off ties with someone who is difficult to get along with, because that person is an important partner for you in business or in regaining your health (for instance, a doctor who has incredible expertise but no bedside manner).

Maybe that "weed" in your garden is your relationship with a sibling, in-law, parent, or old friend who has a lot of problems that she shows no signs of resolving anytime soon; yet there is value in maintaining your connection to this person while strengthening your boundaries. The Gentle Gardener will tell you that some "weeds" serve you in ways you may not see at first glance, such as catnip, which keeps bugs away; or dandelion, whose bitter leaves are edible and nutritious. Plant identification is her specialty.

The Gentle Gardener also knows how to prune—to contain a vine that loves to sprawl, to cut back what is not working so that the plant can grow stronger. However, she won't do this work for you. You have to consciously choose to do the pruning. If a situation or relationship is a "weed" you might want to keep, ask for her help. Talk to her, using the following exercise.

Exercise: A Conversation with the Gentle Gardener

Close your eyes. Breathe deeply and slowly. Let your thoughts become quiet and fade into the background.

When you're ready, allow yourself to experience being in your Field of Dreams. . . .

Notice the plants around you. You see the Gentle Gardener, the Spirit of Mother Earth, tending to her patch. What is she doing right now? What does she look like?

Walk over to the Gentle Gardener. Ask her to identify which plants are weeds and what their names are.

What does she show you?

What does she tell you?

Examine her garden. You might ask her, "When did I plant the seed that created this particular weed?" and "Does this one serve any purpose in my life?"

The Gentle Gardener gives you the answers you seek.

You may pull these weeds, gather them, and place them on the compost heap, where they will break down into fertilizer that can be used to nourish other plants. Or you can prune them to contain them so that they don't overrun your garden.

Carefully consider each weed you have discovered. Will you pull it or keep it? What do you need to remove from your life? What boundaries do you need to set in order to prevent your weeds from getting entangled with other plants, choking them and blocking them from the light that would allow them to grow?

The compost heap is magical. Already it is rich with nutrients from the weeds you just tossed there. You can use it to nourish the plants you most wish to flourish in your Field of Dreams.

Tell the Gentle Gardener which ones you would most like to grow. Which are your favorites?

Ask her, "Do you have any advice for me? Is there something I should know about this plant to ensure that it will grow strong?"

Listen for her answer.

The Gentle Gardener will appear anytime in the sacred place—the garden in your mind where you convene with her. You're always invited to connect to her wisdom, feel your trust in her gardening prowess, and plant a seed, infusing it with your intent. Forming an intention is the beginning. Then you can always ask her, "What is the next action I might take to ensure the integrity of my dream-seed?"

The Gentle Gardener within me has taught me about the weeds and the plants of value in my garden. When I consider my own recovery from compulsive eating and my unhealthy relationship to food, I can see how both of the twin sisters have aided me. Once I was able to reclaim the lost bones of a healthy relationship to food and a healthy relationship with my body, and I could find what I was really hungry for, I changed dramatically. Today, I'm in better health, I have more self-esteem, and most important, I have dignity and self-acceptance.

Conversations with the Spirit of Place

If you do Goblin work and converse with the Bone Collector and her sister, the Gentle Gardener, you'll have an easier time avoiding troubled landscapes. But should you find yourself in one of these distressing terrains, know that you have another hidden ally who can be summoned when you take your place in the seat of the Wizard of Awareness: the Spirit of Place, a male or female archetype who personifies the essential energy of the landscape.

This Spirit knows all about your surroundings, light and dark—all their secrets and hidden treasures.

And, very important, he or she knows how you can escape this terrain. Unlike the Goblin's exit strategy, the Spirit of Place's plan will actually work. When you've learned the wisdom of this place, this ally will help you get out. But first, he or she must ease your feeling of being trapped and in danger.

The illusion of fear, created by the Goblin, has you dodging lightning bolts in the darkness of the Storm Fields and struggling to keep your head above water in the currents of the Raging River. You may be pinned under something, stuck in muck, or at the bottom of a pit, feeling that you'll never get out.

What is your relationship to the land, and why is it making you feel endangered? Are you floating helplessly, longing for the comfort of the shore underneath your feet? Are you dangling from a branch overhanging the Raging River, pleading for help to get back onto solid ground?

Are you running for shelter, exhausted by your uphill climb and heavy load, but afraid to set down your knapsack because you think there is no food or water in this desert?

You need to have a conversation with the Spirit of Place, whose secrets are enlightening. The Spirit of Place can point you to the shelter in the Storm Fields; and magically transform you into an eagle that can fly over the Immovable Mountain and seek out a new, more forgiving land.

Be patient, however, because the Spirit of Place knows that once you have the secret to getting out, you're going to be gone in a wink, and he or she may not be quite ready to let you go. There may be something you have yet to learn. Slow down and have the conversation. Agree not to start running once you're placed on solid ground again, or to fly away the moment you're given wings.

Exercise: Dialogue with the Spirit of Place

Focus on your breath, and breathe slowly and deeply until you feel relaxed and your busy thoughts have quieted down. Let a landscape that represents your inner emotions arise in your mind's eye. Allow your senses to take in its sights, smells, and sounds.

Ask yourself:

- "What is the name of this place?"

- "What are the features of the landscape? How am I interacting with the landscape?"

- "When am I in time? Have I been here before? Do I know why I'm here and what I need to do?"

- "Do I know how to escape? Am I ready to leave, or ready to learn? Which do I need to do?"

Now call out to the Spirit of Place. Allow your imagination to connect with the awareness of the being who embodies the essential elements of this place.

Who is he or she? What does this Spirit look like?

Ask the Spirit of Place:

- "What do I need to know about this land?"

- "What must I do?"

- "Have I learned what I need to know?"

- "Is there anything else you can tell me?"

- "May I go now?"

Take your time and listen.

In your journal, write down the answers you've received from the Spirit of Place.

Sam was in a state of shock when he came to my workshop. He'd been laid off from his job with a company he'd worked for since he'd finished school. He'd lost his livelihood and his identity, and he felt he was in a Raging River, being dragged downstream by the pull of forces beyond his control. He was terrified about his finances and his prospects and desperate to keep his head above water. He'd grab an overhanging branch—an "informational interview" a friend set up, or an opening he'd heard about that gave him some hope—only to have it slip through his grasp.

Sam had never been here before and felt he was in grave danger and all alone. The Spirit of Place showed him that through meditating and affirming all his qualities—not just the ones listed on his résumé, but his personal traits—and by practicing mindfulness, Sam could manage his anxiety and open himself up to creativity and have faith in his future.

Although he left my workshop not knowing exactly how he was going to get back on his feet, he'd already found solid ground inside himself. Sam's Map was aligned with Spirit, and he now knew he was walking a different path, out of fear and into possibility. He knew there would be allies and traveling companions along the way now that he had shifted his map. He went home sure that he had the power to create something new for himself—and accepting that he was on an ever-changing adventure.

And so are we all.

Traveler's Notes

- When you lack faith in your ability to heal yourself, to change your beliefs and self-talk, or to break old destructive habits, turn to Spirit.

- Imagine that you're dialoguing with the magical beings on your Map and you'll be interacting with your inner wisdom and that of Spirit.

- The voice of the Goblin, your wounded ego, is filled with fear or anger and has a quality of urgency.

- If you listen to the voice of the Goblin, you can discern whether there is something to be learned from what he has to say. You can discover hidden issues you must address, and the origin of your wound.

- If it's frightening to picture yourself dialoguing with a Goblin, or impossible to imagine that you could express compassion toward him, then envision a more benign (yet still ugly) being that represents your wounded ego.

- The only way to "tame" the voice of the wounded ego is to explore what it has to say. Ignoring it only gives it, and your subconscious thoughts, more power over you.

- You can reclaim any quality or belief about yourself that you lost or were unable to claim in the past as a result of a wounding. Converse with the Bone Collector and she will find and give life to this lost "bone."

- You can refashion this quality or belief to make it easier for you to "own" it today. If you don't wish to reclaim it in its original form, the Bone Collector can help you alter it so that you feel more comfortable incorporating it into your being.

- Converse with the Gentle Gardener and you will discover what seeds you have planted in your Field of Dreams and why some of your aspirations haven't led to the outcomes you'd expected.

- It's okay to retain some of the "weeds" in your garden—the results of relationships and circumstances you've chosen to be a part of—as long as you're aware that you've made the choice to include these challenging people and situations in your life because there is some positive aspect to them.

- Converse with the Spirit of Place in any emotional landscape on the Map and you'll learn the lessons of that experience, as well as how to change your perception and emotions.

~ *Chapter Seven* ~

TREASURES, TALISMANS, AND MEDICINE BAGS

" . . . where you stumble, there your treasure is."

— JOSEPH CAMPBELL

"Courage and perseverance have a magical talisman, before which difficulties disappear and obstacles vanish into air."

— JOHN QUINCY ADAMS

Now that you know how to interact with the Map, it's time to learn about an extraordinary tool that you can use at any time to more quickly transport yourself out of a landscape. It is one you receive through your experiences of suffering, and it reminds you of the magic and meaning of your life. In your darkest hours, know that you're in the process of obtaining just such a magical object: a talisman.

The word *talisman* comes from an Arabic term meaning "initiation into the mysteries." You are called to initiation at several points in your life, to face death—whether it's real or metaphorical. Although all may appear dark, you have to let go of your fear and embrace the unknown, trusting that Spirit is your guide. If you do, your courage will arise and allow you to remain present in what is happening, explore what you can learn about it, and find the buried treasure in even the most stressful landscape.

This treasure is the lesson that can be learned from any experience that drives you to the depths of despair, rage, or terror. Initiation allows you to be born into a new self that can face a grim diagnosis, betrayal, and loss with the sure knowledge that "with Divine help that is always available to me, I can survive this, too." In the Map, you'll find many treasures that can be forged into a magical talisman.

A talisman serves as a touchstone: Finger the smooth surface and you can remember what you learned and overcame. It will glow, and rekindle your courage as you remember that even a humble, simple rock is connected to All-That-Is; and that your courage flows forth from your spirit and from the Great Spirit.

Although we think of talismans as belonging to ancient indigenous people, many of us unknowingly hold on to ones that take the form of everyday objects. It might be an important letter received years ago, fragile from having been folded and refolded, read and reread, as we recalled a triumph and a great lesson, or the sadness and loss that brought us much-needed humility. It might be a ring or article of clothing that represents a challenge we undertook and survived.

Talismans can incorporate wisdom such as "I can say no, with love" or "I am deserving of respect." In AA, alcoholics are given tokens representing the number of days they've gone without a drink, which are inscribed with the wisdom lesson "One day at a time" and infused with the courage of their commitment.

When you're caught in the Storm Fields, squinting to see where you should go and what you can do, or you're wandering the

Corridor of Uncertainty, a talisman brings clarity and answers. In any distressing landscape, it is there for you, ever present in your pocket, ready to remind you that you've already learned the lesson of this place. Touch it and you find the courage to recognize the old issues and discard the discredited thoughts you have rejected previously. Then you can find your way out of this land.

You receive the talisman from the Spirit of Place, who knows all about the shadow and light of the landscape and can show you where the hidden treasure lies—the words of wisdom that will be embedded in the talisman.

Hidden Treasures

No suffering is in vain if you learn something from it. Your talisman is the crystallized form of the lesson that is the hidden treasure in any landscape. The Spirit of Place will gladly bestow this precious gift. However, you can't receive it if you rush through the land, sparing only a cursory glance at your surroundings.

The greatest treasures are hidden and can only be discovered through patience and exploration. In the Sticky Swamp, you must slow down, let things percolate, delegate to others, and let go of your need to "get it all done." Only then will the treasure rise from below the surface of the mud and gleam in the sunlight. You can't force situations. Like it or not, you must work with the landscape and peer into nooks and crannies, walk around boulders, immerse yourself in rivers, or precariously pick your way across a wobbly bridge to get to the other side, where you escape the story of power-lessness and step into a hero's journey.

Exploring a landscape takes time and, as I said, patience. When you're in trauma, you naturally want to escape it and not spend too much time thinking about it, or risk further suffering by looking at what role you inadvertently played in creating the scenario. Emotionally, you may not be ready to see what is evident when the Gentle Gardener shines her harsh light on the Field of Dreams you've planted and points to ugly weeds you must own as yours.

If shame and self-loathing arise in you when you look at your garden, it's because the Goblin is whispering into your ear, "You see what you did? It's all your fault!" He'll keep you on the run, and you'll exhaust yourself trying to escape the knowledge that your head knows but your heart isn't ready to accept. Feel the support of the Spirit of Place and the love of the Gentle Gardener as you open yourself up to the lesson. Your courage is here for you, waiting to be claimed.

Exploring the Landscape

What do you have to do in your troublesome landscape to find the treasure? Stop running, or get moving? Like the mythical characters Odysseus, Perseus, Hercules, and Psyche—all of whom had a to-do list of chores that only a taskmaster God could possibly dream up—you might need to take action and remain present with your emotions as you come to understand the nature of this emotionally troubling landscape.

Do you have to sail across treacherous waters between a rock and a hard place, as Odysseus did? Like Perseus, do you have to kill off something monstrous that threatens to turn you to stone and prevent you from moving forward?

Maybe you have to climb uphill, wade through mud, clean the muck out of some stables, find a magic potion, or dig in the ground to find water. Perhaps you have to go to the metaphoric local tavern and look for the crone who can help you, and purchase her wisdom by sharing a secret that you've never told a soul.

Enter into your own internal landscape, let your imagination show you the details of your magical journey, and learn from the symbols that spring up from within you. The answer lies within and will not be withheld from you. Engage your talent for active dreaming and your soul will show you all you need to know.

Discovering the Wisdom Lesson

The lesson of the place is always infused with the essence of courage. Mere words aren't enough to create a powerful talisman.

I didn't understand that until I tried to get ahead of myself instead of living one day at a time, and realized that by rushing the future, I was missing the triggers in the present that could pull me back into drinking. "One day at a time" sounds like a simple way to live, but it's not easy. That's the nature of these wisdom lessons: they are far more powerful and valuable than they appear on the surface, and you only learn this when you take the words into your heart.

Allan had attended one of my seminars, where I introduced this process and invited the participants to find a symbolic talisman in their landscape. He had come because he was conflicted about his job and knew he needed to head in a different direction. Yet he couldn't get in touch with his feelings, so he was lost and unsure what to do.

He shared an amazing landscape description with us. I give people three minutes for the In-Vizion process exercise and then ask them to share what they experienced. Active dreaming is much easier than one might think. Allan didn't think he would "see" anything but experienced a profound shift.

He saw himself in a barren desert, chased by wild dogs and running toward the edge of a cliff. As he looked out across a cavernous divide, he saw a magnificent lush green landscape with fruit-bearing trees. When he allowed his imagination to play with this image, he asked to be shown what he was missing. How would he get to the other side? He went right to the edge, then looked down and saw a ledge with beautiful stone steps that led down into the cavern and up the other side. Above him eagles came and dropped water bottles. He took a leap of faith.

All symbols are universal, so since the dog represents loyalty, wild ones snapping at Allan's feet represented the danger of untamed, unbridled loyalty: a form of codependence. The birds were messengers of the soul. His talisman was faith that the life-sustaining water they brought would be his if he were willing to jump to the ledge. The stairs meant he would have to take the next leg of the journey one small step at a time.

When he returned home, Allan negotiated a deal to work part-time and began taking steps toward establishing a new business, one rooted in his passion, which would eventually lead him to the lush green territory he chose to inhabit.

Acquiescence Alley

In any landscape, the Goblin can trick you into believing he knows the magic words that make up the hidden treasure. You might think the lesson is: "At my age, there's no way I'll find the partner I really want, so I'll just settle for being alone or for being with someone who doesn't treat me the way I want to be treated," or "I don't have what it takes, so I won't try anymore. It's just easier than having my hopes dashed again."

These are *not* words of wisdom but words of the Goblin, and they will take you away to Acquiescence Alley. Here, you're banished to the narrow space between high walls and big buildings that you can't enter. In Acquiescence Alley, you have to forage for food from garbage cans; and the only water seems to be the tainted, foul stuff that comes out of a rusty spigot. The whole place stinks and gets you thinking that *life* stinks so you have to take what you can get and settle for less than you deserve.

It seems impossible to get out of Acquiescence Alley, because the Goblin has created the illusion of being caged in. He's done this because he doesn't want you to see that you can walk out of this place and find yourself on the Island of Broken Dreams, where you can reclaim your hope and self-worth. Remember, the Goblin's nature is mischief, and he can only go to sleep if you name him. That means you need to identify him in your more difficult landscapes, because it's there that he holds the most power.

All of us have to make compromises at times because of the parameters of our Map, but if we overdo it and betray what is most important to us, or we resist the reality of our situation, we end up in troublesome terrain. There, we experience the pain of our disappointment and frustration, but we also have a chance to learn what other avenues we might take and what other options are available to us.

Many women I've met in my intensives have this place as their primary landscape. My client Candace arrived with a lot of anger about her life. She'd been in a long and unhappy marriage to her high school sweetheart. She'd gotten pregnant at 19, married, and had three more children. At 42, she felt trapped. Her husband, a very successful businessman, had became addicted to pain pills, pot, and porn. Although he'd cleaned up his act and they'd gone to counseling together, she now realized that her initial compromise to remain home, have kids, and deal with his many issues was no longer acceptable to her.

With no education, financially dependent on her husband, and devoted to her children, Candace came to the seminar not knowing where to turn. She wanted a career but was afraid to go back to school. She was angry and bitter, and the walls of Acquiescence Alley were closing in on her.

She described her internal landscape as an island with too many crowded houses, surrounded by endless water. She went on to describe half-finished paintings and broken pottery strewn along a rocky road leading to a prison. I then asked her to imagine a landscape that could come to her spontaneously to show her the place she felt would best represent what her life might look like if she were happy about her circumstances. I suggested that she not look beyond the temporary confines of her "island."

Candace said that the new place looked very different. There was space between the houses, and the trees on the island all had artwork hanging from them like Christmas-tree ornaments. There was a large boat at the end of a pier, and her children were seated inside of it, wearing graduation gowns and waving to her.

She said that seeing this place told her exactly what she needed to know. Over the years, she'd become very good at crafts and pottery. She didn't have to go back to school! She could create a business around designing and selling Christmas ornaments. Never having considered this possibility before, she was experiencing an epiphany. She could be independent after all. She also knew that her resentments were what was keeping her feeling trapped. She still had a long way to go, but at least she knew where to begin breaking out of her emotional prison and her marital situation.

When you've uncovered a hidden treasure and taken the wisdom into your heart, your work isn't done. You have to create new beliefs that are in sync with this acquired wisdom, and reinforce them through repetition. Otherwise it's too easy for the Goblin to weasel into your awareness and take you back to the thinking you engaged in before you learned your lesson and molded your courage and wisdom in a talisman. The Goblin is a pickpocket who loves to steal talismans, so be forewarned—and make a point of replacing your old habitual beliefs.

You Don't Have to Wear Your Talisman Around Your Neck

You might think of your talisman as an amulet that wards off fear. It's certainly valuable, but you don't have to don it at all times. To "wear" a talisman is to identify with your past experience, to perceive yourself as a survivor of the Raging River, to have your limited notions about yourself hanging around your neck.

Be proud of your triumphs, but don't be weighed down by an incomplete definition of who you are. You are not your past experiences. You incorporate them into who you are, but then you step into something new.

I don't revisit my past, although I refer to myself as a recovering alcoholic and a rape survivor as part of my work, to show others how it's possible to change. I'm proud of having survived those experiences and overcome my limited ideas about myself, but I don't wear them as "wounding signage." None of those things have roots in my landscape now. There are no victim weeds to pull.

My courage and wisdom are crystallized now, and I can wear that talisman or slip it into my pocket. My experiences do not define me, so I don't need that identity of "survivor" or "victim" to precede me into the room. I take out my talisman when I feel the need to reconnect with my courage and share it with others so that I can help them find their own.

A talisman should never be a fetish. All of us have more than one story and one identity.

Flatville

On the Map, there is a land called Flatville. All the buildings have one "story," and all the people are two-dimensional, like paper dolls: this fellow is a bad guy, that woman over there is a saint, and that poor kid never gets a break.

Everyone in Flatville speaks in sound bites. They think they understand one another, but they don't because no one says anything of substance. They write simple, superficial stories and project them onto flat-screen TVs that can be found everywhere. People in Flatville love television because it simplifies everything into a familiar narrative that makes them feel good.

You get to Flatville when you don't want to experience the discomfort of looking more closely at people or events, or because your own insecurities are tugging at you. In Flatville, you can avoid painful emotions and conflicts. No one will contradict you, because here, whatever you say, you're right, as long as you stick with your story. And yes, that is the Field of Poppies at the edge of town. You'll find yourself drifting over there quite often.

You enter Flatville out of fear, when you listen to the Goblin who says, "See? I told you that you can't trust people like that," or "All those people stick together; they don't care about anyone else, so don't expect them to help you." You also enter it when you resist exploring who you might be outside your usual role in your life's stories. You walk around Flatville telling others about your past and never explore what else you might be besides the person you were back then.

There is danger in the single-story, too, as it's so easy to reduce everyone to a stereotype, thereby robbing them of their depth and their humanity. How often do you hear prejudiced comments such as "All blondes have more fun," "Arabs are terrorists," "Psychics are frauds," "Africans are poor," "Black people have rhythm," "Lawyers are dishonest," and "Germans are cold"?

Sometimes Flatville stories are more personal, but they're just as flat—for instance, "My mother was cold and nasty, and my father was abusive and unavailable." When I describe patterns of people's lives in readings, I tell them that you can't honor the complexities of a human being in such a short time, so any statements I make are simplifications.

From Flatville, it can be a quick trip to the Ghostlands of nostalgia unless you speak to the Spirit of Place, who will direct you to a pair of 3-D glasses. As you start to recognize that your mother did her best given her own disappointments and lack of self-esteem, you also begin to acknowledge how uncaring or insensitive you were to her. The story becomes more complex.

With this new, 3-D vision, you see that your ex wasn't such an ogre, and you weren't the perfect prince or princess. That's when you know you can leave Flatville and carry with you the courage to see in three dimensions, with compassion for all, including yourself.

Without compassion for yourself, you may avoid difficult truths for a long time and find yourself departing Flatville, only to enter another unpleasant terrain. It takes a lot of self-love to look at the role you played in the painful situations of your life. You may need to get to Rock Bottom to find what you're missing, for this dark pit of despair is a place where humility cracks open the heart to the light of Spirit and Divine, unconditional love.

Rock Bottom

At Rock Bottom, you surrender to Spirit and open your eyes to the fact that you can't do it all no matter how hard you try—that you're a co-creator with Spirit and must accept that you aren't in control of every aspect of the journey. It's possible that you won't enter the deep pit of Rock Bottom until you've been carried over many traumatic lands. You've probably struggled in vain to avoid them, attempting to spend all your time in the restful and enriching ones. However, if you're suffering, you'll find yourself there one day.

As painful as it is to admit to powerlessness, it's also liberating. By letting go, and relinquishing your power to Spirit and Divine guidance, you find true strength, courage, and self-worth. That jewel of wisdom—that you must surrender to a Higher Power—is a precious gem that is yours to claim at any time, but many of us need to hit Rock Bottom in order to do so and truly accept that Spirit is in charge, not us.

Once you surrender to Spirit, your magical allies will appear. I know they did for me when I stopped living a life of drinking, drugs, and promiscuity and finally accepted that, like Frodo in *The Lord of the Rings,* I couldn't handle the ring of power. The Spirit of Place helped me spot the wisdom and forge a talisman, and I regained my dignity. I was so grateful to the Bone Collector for bringing back what I thought was forever lost that I offered to pay her for her kindness. I showed her the huge diamond I now had in my pocket, a reminder that I'd never have to fall that low again. But the kindly old woman shook her head. She told me that she wouldn't accept anything from me, for her job was simply to return what was rightfully mine.

Again, you don't have to go down the path of addiction, as I did, to hit Rock Bottom. For example, my client Diana was so disturbed by the BP oil disaster in the Gulf of Mexico that it caused her to visit her own Rock Bottom and look at the way she was living her life.

Diana was ambitious, hoping that her dream of becoming an actress would make her rich and famous. Although it sounds clichéd, she moved from a small town in Minnesota to Los Angeles to get "discovered." After a number of failed opportunities and casting-couch disasters, she met a man at a hotel bar. He was handsome, rich, married, and abusive. She spent seven years in this relationship, hoping he would change, trying to be the woman of his dreams. He had no interest in leaving his wife, and gave Diana expensive gifts after each round of abuse. Her auditions led nowhere, so she clung to him, thinking he would be able to give her the life she believed she was meant to have; after all, he was a powerful man, and she was able to move around in moneyed circles. She was admittedly trapped in a prison with velvet handcuffs, never feeling like there was enough of anything, always dreaming of the day when things would change.

Yet when the Gulf oil disaster lingered for months, she looked at her life and realized that her pursuit of fame, power, money, and prestige was alienating her from anything with meaning. Her lover would never leave his wife, and no matter how much money he gave her, Diana was bitter about her circumstances and her failed acting career.

She had just turned 42. One day she woke up and realized she couldn't go on in the same way she had been. She ended the relationship, flew to Florida, and got special training to help clean off the oil-covered birds. I heard from mutual friends that her life has never had more meaning for her. Perhaps her talisman is the oily T-shirt she wears at the beach with the other workers.

I have several talismans that reconnect me to my courage and wisdom. You, too, can experience talismanic magic and create an object that will remind you of your power, using the following exercise.

Exercise: Create Your Own Talisman

Are there some words of wisdom—a quote, a saying, a proverb, a song lyric—that infuse you with courage whenever you hear them? In a journal, write down those words, and explore why they mean so much to you. What past triumph or triumphs do they bring to mind? What emotions do you experience when you say them aloud?

Close your eyes, and envision the type of object you could fashion that would symbolize these words and the courage they generate in you. Here are some items that my workshop attendees have incorporated into talismans:

- A stone with words or a word engraved on it or written on it

- A feather representing the help of angels

- A crystal that brings clarity, and represents the essence of what was learned

- A felt or cardboard heart representing love and courage

- Colored string or ribbon symbolizing ties to a loved one

- A piece of shiny metal with gold flecks, like pyrite, representing the hard work that went into mining a lesson's treasure

Be as inventive as you like in choosing a symbol. Whatever you create will become a touchstone for your wisdom.

How powerful is this exercise? A recent research study in Singapore showed that people who wrote about difficult emotions they wanted to release and sealed their writing in an envelope reported more relief from those painful emotions than did another group who simply recorded them and put a paper clip on the paper they'd penned their story on. Apparently, simply writing down one's emotions and interacting with the paper in a physical way that had no symbolic meaning wasn't nearly as powerful as symbolically "sealing away" the emotional toxins.*

Create a physical representation of your remarkable journey of courage, keep it at hand, and record in your journal how this exercise has affected you.

*Xiuping Li, Liyuan Wei, and Dilip Soman: "Sealing the Emotions Genie: The Effects of Physical Closure on Psychological Closure," *Psychological Science* July 2010; first published on July 9, 2010, doi: 10.1177/0956797610376653.

The Medicine Bag

While a talisman is like a "get out of jail free" card that can spring you from an emotional prison, a medicine bag serves to help you play that card. The pouch of the ancient indigenous medicine woman contained herbs and roots that she could use when performing her healing magic on herself or others. *Your* medicine bag is symbolic. It is your "bag of tricks" that includes tools and techniques for pulling you out of fear so that you can find your talisman and your courage.

I've learned that when I'm hungry, angry, lonely, or tired, I'm more vulnerable to the kinds of thoughts that lead to destructive behaviors, like eating compulsively, so my "medicine bag" includes protein snacks, deep breathing, conversations with friends, and naps. Yours might include the powerful balm of meditation, or the magical potion of exercise. Cognitive therapy, journaling, using oracle cards, mindful eating—all of these techniques can help you recognize the Goblin's voice and resist the shift into fear, anger, and sadness before you end up in an intense landscape. A little preventive medicine every day will help, too, so don't forget that you have your medicine bag with you, and be sure to take a little of its "tonic" daily to foster your emotional and spiritual health.

Sometimes I'll say to myself, "Goblin!" to remind myself that this creature's voice is seducing me and I have to beware. My husband loves this and participates in my self-evaluation, smiling and asking me, "Goblin?" when I'm giving in to insecurities and old beliefs about myself.

Then it's so much easier for me to say, "Hmm, I'm combative for no reason. Must be that I haven't paid attention to my Goblin and he's driving the bus." I'll take a walk or a swim (another bit of "medicine") and think about whether my Goblin's words have any value to them before I push them out of my mind completely. Or I'll ask myself, "Am I hungry, angry, lonely, or tired?" knowing that if I am, and if I address that problem, the Goblin will quiet down.

Also, a daily self-evaluation or inventory is powerful, healing medicine that can restore harmony anytime you choose to use it. In 12-step programs, Step 10 is: "[We] continued to take personal inventory and when we were wrong promptly admitted it." When you take inventory, you monitor your thoughts, feelings, and behaviors to ensure you aren't hurting others or yourself. A "spot check" throughout the day is essential to maintaining inner peace and assuring that your response to life isn't a Goblin reaction. Any question or activity that slows down your emotional response and helps you gain clarity is strong medicine, too.

What "medicine" is in your medicine bag? Sometimes we forget all these tools available to us. The following exercise will help you remember what medicine is at your fingertips.

Exercise: "Assemble" a Medicine Bag

Think about all the techniques you've been able to use successfully to avoid an automatic negative reaction, such as strong anger, deep disappointment and pessimism, melancholy, cynicism, or fear. All of these states of mind compromise your emotional well-being; what medicine works to ward them off? List as many kinds as you can in your journal. Include remedies you haven't tried yet but which you've heard might work for you. Are you willing to try some new techniques?

Maybe your medicine is a way of setting boundaries. Do you walk out of a room or hang up a phone gently when someone begins to be abusive? Think about which words snap you back into a positive mind-set. Perhaps you say, "It's all good," "This or something better is waiting for me," "Breathe; everything's going to be okay," or another affirmation or catchphrase that keeps you standing on solid ground instead of flying through the air, your wrist in the clenched hand of the Goblin, headed toward a distressing landscape. If so, write it down and say it aloud.

You might make a card you carry with you that reminds you of what is in your medicine bag. Here is a sample of one that provides instant medicine. On it are written the words to the Serenity Prayer, plus three empowering and healing statements:

> God, grant me the serenity to accept the things I cannot change;
> the courage to change the things I can;
> and the wisdom to know the difference.

> "What is for me will not go past me."
> "Rejection is God's protection."
> "Spirit is the source of my supply."

It's easy to forget that you have this powerful medicine available to you at all times. Take some every day to build up your immunity to the seductive voice of the Goblin. Create a card for your wallet and repeat these affirmations, or invent your own. What you say is powerful. Speak the words above aloud throughout the day. You will be amazed by their effect. It's like popping a Valium into your Goblin's mouth!

Traveler's Notes

- A talisman is the crystallized form of the wisdom lesson that can be found in any emotionally distressing landscape.

- Every talisman is infused with the power of courage, because it took courage to learn the difficult lesson of the land.

- No suffering is in vain as long as you learn from it.

- Courageously explore your emotional landscape and you'll find the lesson hidden there.

- Acquiescence Alley is the place you visit when you settle for less than you deserve instead of resolving to explore an emotionally challenging landscape.

- Talismans are touchstones, not millstones around your neck. You don't have to identify with the experience that caused you to earn the talisman. You can move on to new experiences and let go of your old identity while retaining your courage and wisdom lessons.

- You visit Flatville when you perceive yourself and others through a limiting lens and don't account for the complexity of how people think, feel, and act. With courage, you can learn to see your role in any situation, and the positive aspects of someone you feel has treated you badly.

- You may have to visit Rock Bottom to learn a lesson. In the pit of despair, there is always hope and courage to be found, because loving, compassionate Spirit is always there for you.

- You have a medicine bag of techniques that helps you find your inner strength and temper the voice of the Goblin.

- Use the "medicine" or techniques in your medicine bag regularly to foster your well-being.

Part III

THE MAGIC AND MEANING OF THIS ADVENTURE

Chapter Eight

WHY ARE YOU ON THIS ADVENTURE?

"I have found that you do have only to take that one step toward the gods, and they will then take ten steps toward you. That step, the heroic first step of the journey, is out of, or over the edge of, your boundaries, and it often must be taken before you know that you will be supported."

— DIANE K. OSBON

"No pessimist ever discovered the secrets of the stars, or sailed to an uncharted land, or opened a new heaven to the human spirit."

— HELEN KELLER

If the Map is the road map of a life adventure, what is it you seek as you journey forward?

Why are you here? What is the purpose of this grand adventure?

In harsh landscapes, we're sometimes so caught up in trying to escape the danger we perceive that we don't ask ourselves these bigger questions. But in the quiet moments as we walk along the road, looking around us, in front of us, and behind us, we start to wonder about our life purpose.

People everywhere are on a quest for freedom from suffering, loneliness, and sadness. They want to feel that whatever suffering they do experience, at least it has a purpose. And they want to be recognized by others, to be seen and valued.

People also want to feel that disaster is not going to befall them and that they have people they can count on. At this time in human history there is so much upheaval that pessimism about the future is rampant. Seeing outer conditions rapidly changing and structures of security falling quickly, we can easily forget we're not alone in feeling that the ground beneath our feet is unstable. Belonging, love, community—all of these offer a sense of security when the cold winds blow and we feel unsure and vulnerable.

Yet human nature also compels us to seek something better even when life is pretty good. Like nature, we are meant to evolve. We seem to have written on our DNA a yearning to create something new, not just in our own lives but in the larger world. Our quest for personal healing is most profound when we understand that addressing our own wounds contributes to the health and well-being of the whole.

Each of us plays a vital role in the evolution of humanity. You matter. We all matter. And when you understand that and embrace that each of us is invaluable to the whole, you recognize that the world is an extraordinary and enchanted place and you always have the ability to co-create something even better. Once you've climbed up into the seat of the Wizard of Awareness, the magic and the meaning begin to reveal themselves.

Five Basic Human Desires

Not long ago, I decided to survey some of the people who came to my seminars to get a sense of their goals. I asked them, "If you could have it all, what would 'all' be?"

Some people were looking for a committed partnership with a lover and a chance to have children, others longed for a return to health, and some said they wanted to feel that they made a difference in the world . . . all different answers, yet everything they sought could be boiled down to five basic desires: *love, security, meaning, creativity,* and *joy.*

These desires are interrelated. There's a sense of security that comes when we're open to new ideas and unafraid of change, when we approach life with an innovative spirit and trust that this openness will lead to better circumstances. We're happy and feel a sense of purpose when we believe we're making a difference in the lives of others. Love provides us with a sense of belonging and security that allows us to take risks and be creative with our lives.

Why are so many people discontent, and disappointed by how their lives have turned out or where they are on the path? Why do so many feel that the world is barren and desolate, a battlefield instead of a land filled with magical, loving allies and opportunities for grand adventure?

I think it's because we focus too much on problems and "fixing" ourselves and the world around us, and don't see the incredible beauty of the human experience. Then, because we look at life in such a limited way, we listen to that tricky Goblin, who gets us to mistake the symbols for the real deal. When we allow ourselves to see beyond the mere trappings of joy or security and reach for what is genuine, our lives become enchanted and filled with possibilities.

Let's look more closely at these five desires and why we fall for the false versions of them instead of embracing authentic love, security, meaning, creativity, and joy.

The Desire for Love

People seek romantic partnerships, friendships, and better relationships with children and family members. Many are able to experience unconditional affection through a bond with a pet, or animals they work with, and wish for more of that sort of love in their lives. Instinctively, they know that love is an elixir, a magic potion that nourishes us and transforms us into something better.

The quest for love will make us anxious and discontent if we don't understand the nature of *genuine* love and instead chase after hollow symbols of it. To be loved isn't to be showered with validation and catered to like a spoiled princess living in a Golden Palace of Wealth, who receives constant admiration or sexual attention. If we think we're entitled to that selfish experience, then true love will elude us.

What's more, in the West we've focused too much on romantic love over that of our fellow man or friends and family. This feeling is expressed in *all* our relationships, within our smaller community and our interaction with the world. But we can end up taking it for granted when we're without a romantic partner, or the marriage or relationship with a lover isn't going well. Then we cling harder to the partnership instead of considering all the love that *is* in our lives, supporting us and holding us up. In an abusive relationship, one partner makes sure the other is isolated from friends and family who can offer unconditional caring that the person isn't getting. With self-esteem battered, the isolated partner takes up residence in Acquiescence Alley.

In the pursuit of love, we can end up buying into the notion of a trophy husband or wife who makes us look successful but isn't emotionally available to us. I've also seen people look to their romantic partners to complete them, to fill in all the holes in their self-esteem and meet all their emotional needs. No relationship can bear this much pressure.

Love floods our hearts when we open up to it in all its many forms instead of using it to create the illusion of power and security. Love is also something to be expressed through us, not won in a conquest of acquisition. Looking to get it from someone else actually prevents us from knowing it.

The Desire for Security

Because of recent and continuing global financial upheavals, people are more aware than ever of their need to feel that the ground beneath them won't open up and swallow them whole. Even those who know they can count on friends, family, and community to support them in a time of crisis long to create security for themselves so that they don't have to be a burden on others. What's more, they want to feel that they have more than enough and can share their abundance with people they care about, and contribute to causes that matter to them.

Complete safety can never be achieved in the world of our senses, but we have some control over our lives because we're co-creators of the Map—and we always have control over our *perception* of safety.

Knowing that Source supports you through bringing you people and circumstances that will help you—knowing that you're an eternal being with marvelous gifts and the magic to co-create a better life for yourself—is the real security. Faith in the guidance of Spirit gives you the courage to take risks, because you're assured that whatever happens, a Higher Power is on your side and you will survive. Spirit provides the allies and the magic wand, but it's your job to let go of any illusions about controlling the world of your senses and climb into the seat of the Wizard of Awareness, where you can easily recognize genuine security.

The false symbols of safety are money and power. We often equate the two and think money will solve all our problems, and enough of it will allow us to live happily ever after. Determined to get to Easy Street, we find that the shortcuts actually take us to other lands, from the Raging River to the Storm Fields.

The Lottery Quick Fix

I met a lovely couple in Europe who had won millions in the lottery. He was an auto mechanic and she was a schoolteacher when they bought their ticket to "freedom." Rather than launching them into a life of happiness, however, this turn of fate ended up separating them from their friends, who no longer shared their lifestyle. At the same time, the couple had a difficult time integrating socially with people who had *earned* their wealth. They were able to travel and buy a lot of what they called "toys," but they were admittedly not satisfied. They were both searching for meaningful work. They were very unhappy, as they felt they no longer fit anywhere. Having it all didn't seem to be "as advertised."

We humans are hardwired to look for purpose and meaning, to create something rather than just park ourselves on Easy Street. We can remain there, content for a while, but then we get the urge to move forward. If we follow that compulsion, we won't find ourselves in the Field of Poppies, letting time tick away as we calcify. Having lots of "stuff" or never having to work again breeds boredom and restlessness.

Materialism as a Substitute for Security, Happiness, and Meaning

Fareed Zakaria, current-affairs commentator and author, points out that even as we in the West are waking up to the futility of pursuing happiness and security through ownership, people in developing countries in the East are beginning to embrace those values. It's time for a different quest if we're to survive as global citizens sharing the earth and its resources. All of us need to step back and ask ourselves: How much stuff do we need, and what is the real cost of materialism? How much satisfaction do we get from our possessions?

There's nothing wrong with owning and enjoying beautiful objects, homes, and cars; but if you think these will give you power and security, you're falling for an illusion. In fact, possessions can start to own *you* because you infuse them with so much power.

When my parents lost everything in a business deal, all their friends ignored them as if they had a communicable disease. The friendships clearly were never genuine, and that was a painful truth my mom and dad couldn't face. They never recovered from the social rejection, and for the sake of emotional security, clung to the fading symbols of their wealth. They couldn't imagine creating a new life for themselves, or finding peace and contentment without being well-off. From them, I learned that genuine security exists only at the center of your being, and that you have to wear the world as a loose garment.

Become obsessed with money and possessions and you'll find yourself trapped in the Golden Palace of Wealth, which is perched precariously over a vast gulley and has its front door guarded by a snooty butler who doesn't want to let you into the party inside. Ashamed and angry, you debase yourself by offering him greater and greater bribes that represent the sacrifice of all that has true meaning for you.

The lesson of this place is that the real wealth that never slips away lies in the garden out back, the Field of Dreams tended by a humble gardener whose ordinary appearance is deceiving. Turn your back on the butler and the glittering allure of the Golden Palace and discover the real riches that await you in the magical garden.

Keep in mind that real goodies are born of the seeds of gratitude. Prosperity is an attitude and a perspective. Now more than ever, you and I and everyone else need to remember this. What you value, what thoughts you think and beliefs you hold, will determine the riches in your life.

The new shape of wealth is hidden in our intentions and the actions we take to manifest them. The seeds aren't found in platinum bowls inside the Golden Palace, but in the rich, dark earth outside it that is waiting to be tilled with love and compassion.

Going Home

Did you ever wonder why Dorothy had such a need to go home as soon as she got to Oz? She landed in a fascinating and colorful place. Why the longing to get back to dreary Kansas? . . . Well, because, to her—be it ever so humble—that Kansas farm was her *home*.

So, too, do *we* long for home even as we venture forth into new experiences and discoveries. We want the touchstone of home, a place where we know we're loved, where we belong, where we're happy. It's a place of safety where we muster our courage, a sanctuary that serves as a base for our adventures, risk taking, and creativity.

Wherever you travel, you can always go "home" if your home is a state of mind rather than a physical place. On the Map, home is under the Resting Tree by the Tranquil Lake. It is also in the Enchanted Woods where all the trees that confound you part to reveal an open space under a big blue sky, and perhaps even an enchanted cottage with a fire in the hearth where you can sleep peacefully for a while. Then, when the opportunity for adventure calls or your circumstances suddenly shift, you must leave, but you can hold on to the knowledge that home will be there for you again, for it is always within you.

We have to be at home in the world as well, free of fear. We can do this when we're at home within ourselves, in our own skin and our own experiences and thoughts.

The Desire for Meaning

We all want to make a mark in some way and to feel that we matter. We want to be able to look back at our lives and feel we did the right thing and lived with integrity. We aspire to be special, to be seen and to see ourselves as an integral thread in the fabric of life and in the tapestry of our larger community.

Only through Spirit can we discover our genuine purpose and the meaning of our lives here on the Map. When we try to figure it out without Spirit's guidance, we fall prey to narcissism and the belief that our job is to amass as much security for ourselves as possible and build up our power so that we can influence others and get them to conform to our plans.

Narcissism, rooted in fear and insecurity, makes us control freaks. It's a distorted way of perceiving that never leads to genuine happiness, love, security, or meaning; and it's no foundation for creativity. Being preoccupied with ourselves is harmful not just to others but to ourselves.

If you listen to your Goblin, you'll start to believe that your life won't mean anything unless you make a huge mark on the world and everyone knows about your accomplishments. Remember, the Goblin represents your wounded ego that longs for validation, so he is desperate to convince you of his own importance. You don't have to become an international celebrity who has solved some major flaw in the human condition to make a difference. You can become well known and have a lot of influence, but it won't necessarily make you happy or help you find your purpose. There are people who are famous just for being famous, such as the folks on reality TV shows. Some of them may be completely lost when it comes to knowing why they're here and where they're going.

Fame, power, and admiration from the masses—all of these are hollow symbols of a life of meaning. Go for the *genuine* meaning. The respect and attention you think will fulfill you will follow, and you'll probably find that it doesn't thrill you nearly as much as the fact that you feel a sense of purpose in your life. I've gotten to know a number of celebrities personally; and the ones who are the most healthy, well-rounded people became famous along the way while working and loving their craft. No one had it easy, either. Be like them: love your life, find meaning, and commit to whatever you do with gusto.

From the seat of awareness, your eyes open up to how truly remarkable you are. You can summon the allies who will provide you with the insights that take you to the path of your destiny, where each of your steps is purposeful.

The Hero's Journey

You might think of your quest for meaning as your own hero's journey. Joseph Campbell, the author of *The Power of Myth,* explained that the hero's journey is the mythological story of our common quest, a story that explains why we suffer and sacrifice. In the grand myths about heroes—from the tales of King Arthur and his knights of the Round Table, to the Greek myth of the trials of Hercules, or even the struggles of Luke Skywalker in *Star Wars*—the quest is for healing and purity, a cleansing of the ego's lower desires.

In some traditional stories, the hero's successful journey culminated in finding the *graal,* also known as the Holy Grail. This was a symbol of purity, creativity, power, and abundance. The graal was also depicted as a horn of plenty or a magic cauldron that provided endless gratification of one's deepest desires: love, wealth that represents security, and so on.

In other stories, however, the hero's journey was an adventure with great challenges that led him to a lake, the source of abundance, where he could heal his wounded soul and then return to his village with the healing waters for the benefit of all.

So at the core of any quest for meaning is the desire to believe that our struggles matter and that we affect the world for the better, and that if we live with integrity, we'll achieve the abundance and healing we desire. Without an understanding of why we have to suffer, we resist and resent all suffering, which only causes us more emotional trauma. Finding meaning frees us from a futile struggle against the parameters of our map and allows us instead to embrace the magic and the mystery.

Now more than ever, the evolution of our entire species depends upon our recognizing the holism of the human experience: that our personal healing contributes to the healing of all, and that prosperity is shared. The cauldron, graal, or horn of plenty we seek is the endless supply of nourishment that provides enough for everyone. Spirit is the source of that endless supply, the invisible force that moves unseen within the world of form.

Whether you think you're searching for God, safety, security, love, happiness, purpose, power, forgiveness, or some kind of peaceful reconciliation within yourself, the hero's journey takes place inside you, on the Map, and affects the lands you traverse in the world of the senses. You find the Holy Grail by looking within, where you can access Spirit.

The magic of Spirit opens your eyes to the truth: where love can be found, where your true source of security lies, what your real purpose is, and how you can create a better life by working with the flow of life itself instead of swimming against the current. Love, security, and meaning come in forms you didn't expect.

The Trap of Narcissism

Be forewarned that in your search for meaning, the Goblin can mislead you into regarding your personal experiences as all-important and worthy of being endlessly analyzed and mined for evidence of your own value. It's possible to turn so far inward that you become self-centered, oblivious to those who travel the path with you.

Too much reflection is blinding. It causes narcissism, wherein you may be able to see your wounds but not your power, and you may find yourself writing stories about how you were victimized rather than taking responsibility for your actions, consciously choosing to change, and empowering yourself. If this happens, you'll get stuck in Flatville.

The term *narcissism* comes from the Greek myth about Narcissus, an arrogant youth who was cursed by lovers whom he spurned and, as a result, fell in love with his own reflection in a still pool. Narcissus reached out toward the image of the beautiful youth he longed to embrace—but he did so in vain, for it dissolved each time his hand struck the placid waters. Narcissus despaired and raged, and finally died after beating himself up in frustration. This is exactly what happens to us when we become obsessed with ourselves for any reason.

None of us can find love or joy living inside our own heads, focused exclusively on "me" and never the "we," seeing only our victimization and not our power. And while the type of self-worship Narcissus practiced afflicts some, just as often people become narcissistic because they are filled with self-loathing. They can't stop thinking about their failures and problems. Their anxiety about their inadequacy overwhelms them, and they can think of nothing but how awful they are. They may commit to a course of self-improvement, but with such little regard for themselves, they become obsessive about their perceived flaws. When presented with evidence that they might have been too self-absorbed when relating to others, they feel even worse, and turn further inward toward depression and anxiety.

For example, when I was drinking, I had no ability to think about anyone's needs other than my own. I was too needy myself. And whenever I recognized that I was being selfish, I couldn't stand the guilt and turned to the bottle yet again.

We have to look past ourselves, and the stories we tell ourselves about what happened to cause all our problems, and instead look below the reflection and plumb the depths of our emotional waters. The Goblin will try to trick us into constantly thinking about our flaws. He knows that if we recognize that it is his voice telling us we're no good—if we discover and confront him, then name and tame him—he'll lose his power over us. Thus, he keeps that negative self-talk going to prevent us from taking the seat of awareness and opening our eyes to our authentic nature as beautiful souls who have the power to co-create a new reality.

If you sense that you've been focused too much on yourself and your problems of late, you may have been lulled by the Goblin. Don't wait for this trickster to whisk you away to an emotionally challenging landscape. Let go of your fear and engage in dialogues with those inner allies and challengers who can help you look beyond your problems and see yourself as beautiful and worthy despite the growth you still need to do.

The Desire for Creativity

People want to contribute, to do something different and new, to offer something of value to others and help alleviate some of the problems that face all of us. The drive to create leads people to have children, mentor others and watch them blossom, improve various situations, and become better human beings. The creative drive is the soul's deep longing for evolution and growth.

Although not everyone is an artist, we're all born with the desire to create. If you don't believe it, think back to your childhood. What did your imagination cook up when you were running through the backyard or hiding out in your secret, magical fort made of blankets and chairs? How rich were the adventures of your dolls or stuffed animals, of your action figures and the cars and trucks they rode in? What happened to your ability to find the possibilities for play in leaves, stones, sticks, and puddles?

As we get older, we're constantly told to curb our "foolish" games and pay attention to the rules that we're taught at home, at school, and in the community. We're supposed to fit in, so we meet with disapproval when our delightful adventures in fantasy worlds of our own making interfere with the "business" of life. That we might be daydreaming in school because we're bored, or because the teacher has drained all the vitality out of her lesson, isn't considered. We learn that to please others, we have to squelch our creativity as we approach adulthood.

When our school days are behind us, our natural human drive to create and evolve often gets distorted or repressed. Instead of enjoying the process of opening up to possibility and trying out new ideas and behaviors, we want to skip over the mastery of the skills, hard work, and risk required to bring about something of lasting value.

To write this and my other books took an enormous amount of work and reflection. I had to humble myself at times and ask for help, or admit that what I'd written wasn't as brilliant as I'd thought it was when I first penned it. But I was driven to create something of value for myself, and my readers. Yes, I wanted to create a book, but I didn't dissociate the end product from the process, which is always the temptation.

We want to get to the good part right away, but the process of creation *is* the good part. Rushing past it cheats us out of the pride of struggle, mastery, and the excitement of discovery.

Today, many people are feeling that it's time to reinvent their lives, to step out of their comfort zone and express themselves in a new way, to innovate and fashion a life that is very different from the one they've led.

That tricky Goblin will urge you to take shortcuts and focus on the results, but if you listen to him, you'll end up in a Ghost-land of wishful thinking. Remain here in the present, connected to your drive to take a risk. Align with your principles and values, and find security in the support of Spirit. You'll come to know which steps to take.

This is the secret to creating something great, to emerging and becoming rather than just being and doing. You hold the potential to create what you were meant to bring into being. However, you have to stop distracting yourself and talking yourself out of the exciting adventure you experience when you give in to genuine creativity.

The Desire for Joy

The pursuit of happiness is named as an unalienable right in the U.S. Declaration of Independence, because every human strives to achieve this fleeting state and maintain it as long as possible. We often think of happiness and joy as interchangeable, but one is more a pleasant state of contentment, while the other is a deep and profound emotional experience. We know we want happiness, but when we experience joy, we realize just how much more intense an emotion it is.

At the border of any challenging landscape are the Peaks of Joy that offer a perspective you can't find anywhere else. These peaks are at the top of the world, where your heart soars and you experience deep awe at the privilege of being part of such a beautiful enchanted Map. From this vantage point, you can see the interconnections with other maps, the underlying layers that reveal what yours once looked like before you made the choice to change.

When I stand on the Peaks of Joy, I can see the geography that replaced the Barren Desert and the other painful landscapes I was lost in for so long. Gratitude fills me when I realize where I was going back when I was trapped in those landscapes. Now I can see all the interconnected, magical layers. I see the people I met "accidentally" who changed my life and would never have crossed my path had I not altered my map. I see the lands I transformed, and I am so glad to be alive and able to experience this marvelous adventure, guided by spiritual allies.

Gratitude and awe transport us to the Peaks of Joy in an instant. Our perspective about everything in life automatically shifts while seeing from this sentry point.

Happiness is fleeting, and our false symbols for it are the things that foster the illusion that everything is going great and therefore we're content and always will be. But genuine happiness occurs within us regardless of our circumstances—and we can be happy by choice. Micromanaging our circumstances or parking ourselves in front of the TV or inside of the status quo, chugging along doing exactly what we've always done and never striving for more, does not provide the happiness we're looking for. It certainly doesn't get us close to joy.

Westerners, in particular, have been taught that happiness can be purchased at the mall or, better yet, through "this special TV offer" (and, as I mentioned, now such values are being spread to other areas of the world). In the West, we seem to want only what is shiny and new, what promises to make us look younger and be more attractive to potential lovers. We want what will provide us with a sense of security, a sense of belonging, and we convince ourselves that the advertisements are correct: money can buy happiness.

Actually, financial advisor Jean Chatzky, the author of *You Don't Have to Be Rich,* polled 1,500 Americans and discovered that people who made more than $50,000 a year weren't necessarily any happier than anyone else.

Genuine happiness and joy are found when you let go of your limited notions about what circumstances will make you happy and choose instead to see the world as an enchanted place. Purpose, security, love, and belonging—and the ability to evolve—are part of your birthright. To claim them, you need only to find the magic. It's there, on the Map.

Traveler's Notes

- We are all on a quest to achieve five basic, interrelated human desires: *love, security, meaning* or *purpose, creativity,* and *joy.*

- When we listen to the Goblin, we grab at false symbols of what we desire.

- False symbols of love include relationships rooted in dysfunctional dynamics, where one person has power over the other, or one person expects the other to provide him or her with status.

- False symbols of security include money and power. Much of the materialism today is rooted in the desire for safety.

- Another false symbol of safety is clinging to our identity as part of a group to meet the need for belonging.

- Genuine security can only be found within, where we connect to Spirit, not outside of ourselves.

- Ultimately, we are all here on a hero's journey toward healing—the healing of ourselves and the larger whole of humanity.

- Narcissism and self-importance are false symbols of meaning. We should examine ourselves but not obsess about ourselves.

- Genuine creativity eludes us when we look to shortcuts and refuse to do the difficult work of being open to possibility and persevering when the road is challenging. Then we end up in a Ghostland of wishful thinking.

- Our false symbols for joy are those things that foster the illusion that we can be permanently happy and avoid all suffering.

- Trying to control everyone and everything around us doesn't lead to genuine happiness, which is only found when we surrender to Spirit.

- By quieting the Goblin's voice, we recognize that we can "have it all"—that is, achieve these five basic experiences that humans desire.

- Spirit wants us to find love, security, meaning, creativity, and joy; and works with us to help us have those experiences.

Chapter Nine

FINDING
THE MAGIC

*"The magical approach takes it for granted that the
human being is a united creature, fulfilling purposes in
nature even as the animals do, whether or not those purposes
are understood. . . . The magical approach takes it for granted
that each individual has a future, a fulfilling one, even though
death may be tomorrow. . . . Overall, that approach operates in
your world. If it did not, there would be no world. If the worst
was bound to happen, as the scientists certainly think, even
evolution, in their terms, would have been impossible."*

— SETH, VIA JANE ROBERTS

*"This world, after all our science and sciences,
is still a miracle; wonderful, inscrutable, <u>magical</u>
and more, to whosoever will <u>think</u> of it."*

— THOMAS CARLYLE

THE MAP

So, now that you've begun to explore your inner world through the Map, can you find the magic and meaning in the story of your life? Can you see that no matter where you are, you're never lost, that there's always movement and something new to discover?

Imagine . . . the Map is spread out in front of you, and you have a chance to observe your journey thus far:

The Wizard of Awareness hands you his wand, and motions for you to take a seat. Observe from this vantage point how you have traveled long and hard through various landscapes—some stormy, some rocky, some flat, and some mountainous. You have crossed calm seas and wandered, parched, in the desert. You have traversed difficult terrain and met Goblins in dark places. You have encountered allies such as the Gentle Gardener, who taught you to consciously plant your intentions in the Field of Dreams; and have found your courage and self-worth, kept safe for you by the Gentle Gardener's sister, the Bone Collector.

You've followed the signs after speaking to each Spirit of Place, and collected your symbols of wisdom, hard-won in some cases. You carry their essence with you, and that empowers you on your journey. As your consciousness expands into an ever-greater awareness of your purpose, you sense something shift. Inspiration touches you, and suddenly you find yourself entering a moist green forest saturated with colorful life, rich with the sound of flowing streams.

This vibrant territory hums with the constant flow of continuous movement. Although you've been here many times before, there is much to be discovered, so you continue your journey. You follow the flow effortlessly until you come to a cliff's edge, where a huge chasm separates you from the other side—your next destination, a fulfillment of your dream. You turn around, believing you're in the wrong place, but the landscape behind you has turned into an alley of chaos, with storms and tornadoes. You must press on. But where will you go?

*You sit down under an ancient willow tree to consider. Why
has the flow suddenly stopped? Will the storms catch up and
destroy you? You feel a Goblin stirring, but you're very tired, so
you close your eyes and fall asleep. You enter a dream in which
you are lost in the Corridor of Uncertainty. Which door leads to
the truth? What is real? In your dream, the Wizard of Awareness points his wand—and suddenly, you wake up.*

*Two beautiful songbirds have alighted upon the tree branch
above you. You are in the zone between waking and dreaming,
where your intuition is in tune with their song: "Have faith,
have faith, walk, walk, do, do!"*

*You follow the message and step right off the cliff—but
as you do so, a bridge appears underneath you. You cross to
the other side of the abyss, where the next synchronistic event
awaits.*

*Are you listening? Even the rocks have messages if you re-
main aware, awake, and available. The invisible becomes visible, the formless finds form, and the impossible is possible.*

Magic is the consciousness that pervades all of life and the
infinite order working within all things. Even in what seems to
be chaos, there is order that we cannot see, a force such as mag-
netism, gravity, or electricity that reveals itself through its effects.
You may not be able to find logic or reason—the "how"—for the
magic in the world, but you can know its mystery firsthand. Just
look around you.

You may know that the human body is made up of chemicals
and neurons and other parts. You may know that sex between a
man and a woman produces a child. But you can't intellectually,
logically, or reasonably know how or why the soul animates the
baby, or what role personality has in shaping her destiny. You
can see the evidence of the soul and the personality. You *know*
this is true.

Why, in Dr. Masaru Emoto's experiments, do grains of rice
that are systematically ignored turn to toxic mush over time;
while rice in another jar, told daily "I love you," flourishes into

rich malt? Plants hooked up to a polygraph machine begin registering electromagnetic activity when one of them is threatened. How is this possible?

Everything is consciousness: the universe is alive and filled with awareness. That is the magic we forget, or perhaps never learned how to see. When we're taught that everything is made up of parts that are only valid if they're measured, it's hard to see that soul is everywhere.

That quality of soul, that awareness, is what makes magic come alive and is the true essence of everything from a seed to a galaxy and beyond. Magic is also the evidence of the invisible, ineffable "why." You'll never fully understand it, but you can feel it with every ounce of your own essence. Love is magic and Spirit is magic.

Magic always calls to you. The minute you sense it and are willing to see, hear, and heed it, it will find you.

If you look back over your entire journey to date, I know you'll find evidence of this power. Reflect on how many seemingly chance meetings and coincidences changed your life. Has your intuition ever led you out of logical explanations . . . into inspired revelations?

I've read for thousands and thousands of people over the past 22 years, and I know that the average person is immersed in magic daily. All of us have been "led" by invisible forces that defy reason into circumstances that further the manifestation of a long-held dream. The energy that ignites transformation is what makes the Map of your life enchanted. This magic is in your consciousness, the awareness that you're connected to all of Creation and working with Spirit to transform yourself and the world around you.

Alchemy, Enchantment, and Grace

In medieval times, practitioners of alchemy believed it was possible to turn base metal into gold, or turn base humanity into a higher form of conscious awareness. To turn from fear to love . . .

this is true magic, and it's available to all of us, because we all have the potential to be alchemists in our own lives. We have within us the capacity for metamorphosis, for evolution, for miracles. And when we change, the world transforms as well.

At any time, you can experience the world as enchanted. You need only to step into a different dimension of consciousness, the creative aspect of awareness. As a human being, you've been given the gift of imagination: the ability to conceptualize, to create within your mind. In this realm of reality, you're able to work with the magic that's hidden behind the mundane.

Allow your awareness to include the Spirit within the form that your senses perceive. Look at a tree. You can see how it draws water through its roots, and sunlight into its leaves—how it nourishes itself and grows—but you're also able to see the Spirit of that tree. You become aware of this vital force . . . its very soul. A tree will no longer be just a tree, but a wondrous expression of Spirit that speaks to you. Everyday miracles will reveal themselves to you as you participate in the alchemy that will transform your life.

I remember what it was like for me when I had my first glimpse of the transformative magic of a tree. It was the beginning of January 1986. I was in my second week as an inpatient at a women's drug- and alcohol-addiction treatment center. I had gone for a walk to ponder my fate, wondering how the compulsion to drink and use drugs had been removed. Nothing I had done on my own had worked at all up to that point, no matter how hard I'd tried. Somehow, during those first two weeks, knowing I'd really hit bottom, I'd realized that I had no place left to go. Surrendering to the truth of my circumstances, finally connecting to a Higher Power, and listening to the stories of the other women had worked!

I walked as I always did, without looking in front of me, my mind a jumble; and then my boot heel got caught in the muddy snow. I looked up and saw a silvery birch tree sparkling with icicles. I don't know why, but as I looked at it, I considered that something greater than I was had *made* that very tree, enabled it to be, and was the power that was giving it life. Unable to move, I sensed the magic in the moment. *Maybe the Spirit that created and sustained this tree is also keeping me sober.*

Grace entered me as I recognized that undeserving though I may be, I had the full support of Spirit holding me up. The compulsion to drink and do drugs, which had been my constant fear and my daily nemesis, had been removed as if by magic, never to return. I will have 25 years of sobriety by the time this book is published.

Grace is the magic that happens when you stop flailing about and notice that you're not sinking after all, and that there's potential for reaching the shore. Like a child recognizing for the first time that she doesn't have to fight the water to stay afloat because she is naturally buoyant, you can only experience grace when you slow down and become still. Then you remember how to use your limbs to glide through the water toward the solid shore.

Grace is the ultimate unmerited gift that can change your life completely and open you up to all the possibilities of the imagination. Bring a broken alcoholic at Rock Bottom, filled with shame and remorse, into contact with God's grace, expose her to others who share the same experience and the same desire for a better life, then be assured that the "chemical" reaction is powerful. Transmutation is sure. I'm living proof of it.

In the bigger picture, alchemy is what is happening within all of us at this time in history. We have treated the earth terribly, but I believe with all my heart that we will not destroy our planet or ourselves, because of the magic of Spirit's grace. Grace will let us rise above our fears and become stewards to our home, as we were meant to be. Whatever problems we face will be matched by ideas sprung from the well of our imagination, drawn from the infinite creativity of Spirit. We will be able to tap into the hidden wisdom in our own memory banks and even in the memory bank of Divinity. Then our co-creative magic will flourish, as it always does when we recognize that we are at Rock Bottom and must surrender our fear and our will to our Higher Power.

This co-creative magic is very different from wishful thinking, which remains ethereal and never takes form. Spirit participates in the alchemy when we're willing to take the risk of trying something new, of sailing into uncharted waters, guided by the

Compass of Spirit. Spirit, knowing how easily we forget the support that's available to us, will provide unmistakable signs of its presence.

You and I, and everyone in the world, are invited into this new time of great change as we acknowledge that we're facing the bottom of our addictions to unsustainable practices. We can give in to fear and allow our Goblins to drive our bus over the edge, or we can allow the magic of our inner wisdom to take the next right action for all our benefit. Only by releasing our tight hold on the old can we allow Spirit's magic to run through us to provide us with the courage to change. Then the magic unleashed through the power of deliberate intention sets all manner of events in motion. We don't need to know the details in advance; we just need the willingness. The proverbial Red Sea will part.

All Magic Begins Within

When your mind is calm and neutral and you're sitting in the chair of the Wizard of Awareness, you're able to work with your allies and challengers to create rich, healthy environments in which to grow. You have the power: it resides within you, not outside of you. You steward it from the inside out into the world.

I recently introduced this material at a workshop and did a vision-journey exercise in which the participants would meet the character representing the higher self, or witness: the Wizard of Awareness. Afterward, one of the participants was visibly upset because in her experience, she'd had to *ask* the wizard for the magic wand and get permission to sit in the chair rather than just taking the wand and her seat.

We're so used to being told that the power is outside of us that this reaction is understandable. I pointed out that the wizard was inside of her, because he's a part of each individual's psyche. He's our witnessing self.

Your "magic wand" is the tool of perception, and it is under your control. Consciously choose to shift how you view an event and you'll marvel at how swiftly the light changes and you receive insights. The magic is revealed when you're willing to see that the world is not just a place made up of discrete parts, but that everything is connected and, in fact, the world has a soul.

Anima mundi, the soul of the world, is waiting for us to claim our magic and make a beautiful new home for ourselves on Earth, one person at a time, one small light at a time.

Yearning for Magic in Our Lives

We want our lives to be magical, and they can be if we reconnect with our ability to make magic in conjunction with Spirit. Then we'll be able to let go of the creeping fear that we're all alone, engaged in a monumental struggle against the forces of change.

In fact, when you acknowledge the Spirit in all things, you see that you're always supported, always part of a larger whole that values the unique expression of Divinity that is you. In the movie *Avatar,* the indigenous people, the blue Na'vi, have a sacred relationship to a huge sentient tree called the Tree of Souls, which is their spiritual center. The soul of their planet and their species—the sum total of their memories—is found together, stored within the living Spirit in this tree: Eywa.

Just as the messages expressing our archetypal, universal experience are found in fairy tales and ancient myths, this modern film reminds us how connected we are to each other, to life, to our planetary home, and to the Spirit from which we individuate and to which we return. The memory of all the wisdom and experiences of the Na'vi is cherished, as is every creature in the forest. The parts and the whole are equally sacred.

Participating in Creation means giving up resistance to change, which is the only constant in life, and recognizing that you're part of that ever-shifting living web. By accepting this essential truth, you become aware that you belong to the greater whole that is striving for something better, for the evolution of all people, including you. When you recognize that you're interwoven with all

Creation, you'll find that the higher part of your "self" knows that it is eternal, and your fear of being unimportant falls away as you begin to see your purpose. You cease worrying about the past and future and embrace the present moment, where you play a vital role in the evolution of all, beginning with yourself.

But as a co-creator and a cartographer on the Map, you must learn how to recognize the signs of magic and work with your extraordinary powers. Like Mickey Mouse in the hilarious cartoon *The Sorcerer's Apprentice,* you must be careful what you wish for and use magic not to shirk responsibility and find shortcuts to ease your life, but to bring forth something of great value.

How might this adventure unfold as a result of your newfound awareness of your powers? Imagine . . .

> *Cold and bitter winds are swirling around you. They feel harsh against your face and skin; and you try to brace yourself against them, wishing you had a coat. Much as you strain to see where you are, you can't make anything out because your eyes are still adjusting to the darkness all around you.*
>
> *You hear a crisp, crunching sound as you trudge forward. Is someone there, or are those echoes of your own footsteps? Lights come into view over the horizon. Stars begin to appear in the sky as the night clouds dissolve. You see a constellation that you recognize and think, <u>That's strange. It must be winter.</u> You shake your head, for you were just enjoying the sunshine but a minute ago.*
>
> *And then you remember what happened, the evidence that all is not as it seems. The sun darted behind a cloud, and you suddenly found yourself here, in this Frozen Land.*
>
> *You hear snickering behind you, and turn to see a mischievous Goblin. Knee-high, with huge ears sticking out from his gnarled head, he blurts out, "I told you that you didn't know what you were doing. Ha! Should've listened, should've listened. You don't know anything."*
>
> *His singsong voice rings in your ears as suddenly you remember the moment you were transported when your mood instantly shifted.*

You are numb with shock, unsure of where you are, where you are going. Why are you here in this forsaken land? What is this place?

And then you feel something heavy in your pocket. With numb fingers, you pull it out and peer at its glowing face. It is the magical Compass of Spirit that always points to true north. Although you are shivering, you feel your heart begin to warm. You realize you have allies in this dark and lonely place. Spirit is here, in many guises, holding wisdom for you.

You recall what you need to do. You turn and smile at the Goblin. He has no idea what a powerful being you are, but there's no reason for him to be afraid. Your magic is from Spirit and is always used for good, and you have learned to love this little trickster. You know he thinks he is looking out for you. It's just that he is deeply misguided. It is time to put him to bed.

In this moment, you know where you are: in the wintry landscape of the Frozen Land, where you must practice patience and take time to dream in the crystal cave. "X" marks the spot. You are on the Map and are ready to begin your magical work.

Sometimes it's difficult to believe that magic is always present in life. Perhaps you think yours has run out? The best way to find it is to look at your story thus far. No one runs out of magic. It's impossible. Your capacity to see it depends on your willingness to keep an open mind. The following exercise will awaken you to the magic you've been experiencing.

Exercise: Noticing the Magic in Your Life

In your journal, list five times in your life when seemingly coincidental events led you to an important change. Think about people you met "accidentally," or opportunities you learned about in a most unexpected and unusual way. Describe the circumstances that you couldn't have planned, yet which occurred anyway.

(Here's an example: I finally surrendered to the fact that my music career wasn't going to take the place of my intuitive-counseling practice, and I deliberately prayed: *Spirit, please lead me to my highest good.* Once I did so, I did a reading for a new client in the U.K., who led me to a company that introduced me to my publisher, Hay House . . . which led me here to you. I could never have planned that, nor taken premeditated steps to achieve that result.)

Magic comes most easily through surrender. List five times in your life when surrendering to something gave you peace, which yielded a different perspective.

Spirit indeed works in mysterious ways, but as marvelous as unexpected evidence of magic may be, it's just as wondrous to behold your power to work with Spirit to co-create these miracles. You may not realize that you're doing so because the results haven't been achieved yet, but pay attention. Do you feel that you and Spirit are walking together, in alignment? Do you trust that what you find around the corner will be a delight? Close your eyes and feel your connection to the ultimate magical mapmaker, who is right here with you.

Traveler's Notes

- Magic is the living consciousness that suffuses all of life and the infinite order working within all things.

- Everything is consciousness: the universe is alive and filled with awareness.

- Chance meetings and coincidences that changed your life are evidence of magic at work.

- The magic is in your consciousness, the awareness that you are connected to all of Creation and working with Spirit to transform yourself and the world around you.

- Grace is a form of magic. It is an unmerited gift that opens you up to all the possibilities you'd never have imagined.

- Grace helps you rise above your fear and become a steward in the world, co-creating magic that heals you and the planet.

- Magic works because of the power of Spirit.

- Magic is ever present. You notice it when you alter your consciousness.

- You are part of an interconnected whole. Magic happens when you recognize this truth.

Chapter Ten

WORKING THE MAGIC

"The whole idea of compassion . . . is based on a keen awareness of the interdependence of all these living beings, which are all part of one another and all involved in one another."

— THOMAS MERTON

"Coincidence is the word we use when we can't see the levers and the pulleys."

— EMMA BULL

Reality is a mystery that is always moving. And in this world of the Map, we see the nature of reality as it is expressed in synchronicity, messages of spirit, and so on. The reality we experience when we take off the blinders of logic and emotion is nonlocal, mysterious, and magical.

When you assign weight and meaning to seemingly odd co-incidences such as "chance meetings," *cledons,* and synchronicity, you're able to sense that there's a great hand guiding your journey and that you're being looked after. First, I'll explain just what I mean by these terms, and then I'll describe how they work as a result of the nature of reality. With this understanding, you'll be able to both recognize the magic in your life *and* work with it.

Synchronicity

Synchronicity, a term coined by Carl Jung, refers to a meaning-ful coincidence. If you pay attention to these events, you can see how they're magical moments of protection and clarity. What are the chances that you attract four men in a row who all have issues with their mothers, and all tried to rescue an ex-girlfriend who suffered from depression? Could it be that you're being led by your own desire to rescue your partners, or perhaps by the expectation of abandonment? The magic that is calling you here is the power within you to shift your entire perspective about where you are in the equation and stop reliving the same circumstances, just in a slightly different form.

Let's say you talk to a new potential romantic partner and choose to remain open to all the cues that might alert you to the presence of a train at the station that's just waiting to send you back to an old, traumatic landscape called Codependent Land. At first this guy seems so different from the other men you've been involved with—he's charming, funny, and attentive. Then he says something uncannily similar to what a previous lover once told you—someone with whom you had a painful, dysfunctional re-lationship. It may seem illogical, but you instantly recognize in this seemingly benign, short interaction—in a turn of phrase, accompanied by a particular facial expression—that this person has difficulty handling productive and positive confrontations. You've just experienced a synchronicity. What does this mean? What should you do?

As you recognize the potential to fall back into familiar, painful territory, you may quickly decide that you don't want to "go there" again. By now you know that the Map will bring you someone else—a new lover who doesn't have those unresolved issues and won't pull you back into Codependent Land.

Alternatively, you might decide to consciously and deliberately invite this new person to try having honest, compassionate communication with you. You know that if you choose to be with him, you'll have work to do to make your interactions less dysfunctional. You'll have to be your healthiest self and not "engage" when his behaviors trigger memories of painful relationships. You must take responsibility for the choice you make and act differently this time.

I love the saying "If you do what you did, you'll get what you got!" Remember that the Gentle Gardener waters both flowers and weeds, so if you plant a seed for an unhealthy partnership, she'll ensure that it persists. Is this a plant you want in your garden? Are you growing it because a Goblin has convinced you that you lack the ability to grow anything else?

Listen to the synchronicity and you won't have to board the train to Codependent Land, Enmeshment Village, Acquiescence Alley, or Shouldville (the place where avoidance behavior is the rule and everyone is exhausted by the effort required to walk on eggshells without breaking them). You have the magical power of transformation and transportation. Will you allow something different to take shape with your Map now that you've seen the signpost that says: "Codependent Land, Next Exit"?

Cledons

In my second book, *Messages from Spirit,* I wrote at length about one of my favorite subjects—the cledon. In ancient Rome, if you sought an answer to a vexing question, you would ask the gods, or specifically, the god Apollo, for a sign, then walk to the market square and listen. Inevitably, a random passerby or vendor would say the very words you needed to hear—the words that form a "cledon."

You turn on your radio just at the right time to catch song lyrics that are personally meaningful, or you stand on the subway platform and overhear a conversation between two strangers confirming that the direction you've chosen to take is the right one. Cledons are evidence of magic working as your Map unfolds.

When I do demonstrations of readings from the stage, I'll always say before I begin, "Pay attention. The messages I'm receiving may ultimately be intended for one person, but they might resonate for ten different people who are meant to be awakened to awareness by them. It's possible that *you* will be impacted by what I say to a stranger."

My weekly call-in radio show on **HayHouseRadio.com**® is an even better example of this, as invariably I receive fan mail from listeners who say, "Your message to the lady in Cleveland about her husband was also meant, verbatim, for me!" or "It was as if you were talking about my life throughout the whole show, so I'm writing to thank you so much for your guidance, even though you don't know me!" To work with the magic of cledons, you must listen and pay attention!

I had a startling cledon delivered to me when I was sitting in a café with my husband in Los Angeles. I'd just become a vegetarian and was committed to a cruelty-free diet, but I was unsure about switching from dairy to soy milk. I was feeling much healthier and had found that my readings had been even more accurate and precise than before. Yet as I'm a self-confessed foodie, I was hard-pressed to give up ice cream and cheese.

My husband, Marc, and I were talking about my dilemma when a young father who was with his two-year-old daughter sat down at the table next to us. The little girl gurgled away in her high chair and then announced her new speaking abilities by happily declaring "Boy!" when she saw a man, and "Girl!" when she saw a woman. Her proud father seemed thrilled with her, and praised her for her excellent language skills and budding genius.

I thought she was very cute and smiled at her, but she looked at me and said, "No!" Each time I'd make eye contact, she'd repeat, "No!" Her father looked embarrassed, and I was very confused because really, all babies and puppies love me!

The discussion of my dairy/no-dairy decision went on until Marc finally said, "Look, just ask for a sign." Right then, the little girl turned and looked directly at me and said loudly, with great verbal precision, "Mad cow!" then looked away and returned to her happy gurgling.

Needless to say, with my husband as my witness, I received my sign, and allowed the magic of that moment to solidify my resolve to avoid dairy products. God forbid I would be the source of anger for any more cows! I then was led to purchase a book that very afternoon called *The Face on Your Plate* that "coincidentally" was all about the sad plight of dairy cows in factory farms. I rest my case. Magic answers. Just be prepared for a potentially strange delivery.

Serendipity

Magic also shows up in other unexpected forms and places. Rather than discover what you set out to find, you may instead come upon something wonderful and completely unexpected. Your job is to remain open to it.

The opportunity for serendipity lies in every landscape, in every part of your journey, but only if you remain alert, and aware enough of your environment to recognize it. Serendipity is bestowed upon the curious and openhearted, and reminds you again that what happens on the journey is a magical unseen arrangement of potentials and possibilities.

It's true that we often find the greatest gifts while looking for something else. My client Joe is a great example of this. I had read for him a few times over the years and usually spoke to him about his career path, since it's all he ever wanted to talk about: "When will I make $20 million?" To which I would invariably answer, "I have no idea."

He was always very ambitious and was sure that his banking career was on the rise. His marriage had ended due to his all-encompassing obsession with success. One day he told me he'd just been offered a very prestigious position in a brokerage business. This opportunity was to be his crowning achievement, and he sought validation of that. Yet I saw that his life would drastically change and he would be doing something quite different in a couple of years. Not getting the "right answer," he quickly dismissed me, and I didn't hear from Joe again until three years later when he was on his way to live in Australia.

So what happened? Well, the great job died when the firm he joined collapsed six months later. Due to his association with that company, he was now a pariah in New York. Without prospects, he turned his sights on another country. He'd heard about an Australian banking position through a colleague in Hong Kong, and hoping to restart his finance career, he'd procured an interview in Sydney. He decided to visit an old college buddy he'd remained in touch with who owned a small surfing business Down Under.

When Joe got there and learned a bit more about his friend's enterprise, he offered him all kinds of great ideas about how to expand the business. His friend ended up offering him a partnership.

Now, Joe was still hoping to get that banking job in Sydney, but he told me that he "heard" his own voice saying, "You're done; that's it." He looked in the mirror and decided in a flash that he would agree to the partnership with his buddy and give up his life as a banker. After all, he'd loved surfing when he was young, and he knew a lot about business.

Before Joe moved overseas, he asked me how successful the surfing business would be (naturally). Yet, the magic of his story isn't about his final happiness or achievement . . . it's in the pattern of synchronicity and serendipitous opportunity that he followed. His seeming failure put him into alignment with his true destiny.

I heard from a mutual friend that although he is nowhere near as financially successful as he had been, he's more content than he ever thought possible. He had followed every logical step of the way to fulfill his dream: he went to the right schools, worked his way up the ladder, sacrificed everything for his dream . . . and then it was gone in an instant! Yet, by failing at one dream and then following the clues that led him into unknown territories, he created a life for himself he never could have imagined. He found what he was always looking for, albeit in a very different package. Oh, and I should mention that he married a woman he met in a Sydney café, who, it turned out, was friends with several people he knew back in America—another example of synchronicity.

You can't intellectually understand the magical workings of fate and destiny by analyzing and planning. You have to show up for it by immersing yourself in the experience of being open and receptive to what comes. Even failure and loss can lead to rich, potent new opportunities. Like Christopher Columbus, you may be invited to discover a new land while looking for another. I'm sure *he* wasn't too disappointed.

Magic, Feelings, and Imagination

One thing Joe and I had in common was that we could imagine what our lives would look like when our goals were reached. We knew at a deep level how success was supposed to feel. The essence of what both of us were attempting to create, however, wasn't to be found in the form we expected. My dream of being a successful recording artist touring the world was serendipitously replaced by an opportunity to tour the world as a psychic medium and intuitive counselor. Joe's dream of finding inner contentment in his financial career was replaced by a surf shop in another country, where he married a beautiful woman.

Affirmations are a way of taking what you imagine for yourself and creating seeds of intention that you can plant in your Field of Dreams. They are a powerful way of co-creating with Spirit. The following exercise uses the enchanted landscape of the Crystal Canyon of Echoes to help you let go of old beliefs and ideas about yourself and your life and replace them with new ones.

Exercise: Working with the Crystal Canyon of Echoes

You've been introduced to the Canyon of Echoes previously in this book, but you may not realize that this magical canyon isn't actually composed of rock; it's made of *crystal*. Words reverberate and are reflected back to you, as images that mirror your beliefs appear on the shiny walls. It's here that you can become aware of your inner dialogue and the old beliefs that no longer serve you now that you know better. And it's here that you can replace these old, destructive beliefs with new, empowering ones.

What if you were in this Canyon of Echoes? Take out your journal and describe what words you would hear—words you spoke in the past; ones that reflect your beliefs about yourself, about other people, about life. Don't judge them, or yourself for writing them. Start by simply noting them and jotting them down. Pay attention to the emotions you feel as you write these words. Do you feel ashamed, liberated, puzzled? Record any emotional responses you have to your beliefs.

Are your emotional responses muted or nonexistent? Are these words like mental detritus? Do they only have power when you treat them like found treasures instead of discarded garbage?

Now look at the words you've written and ask, "Are these true for me now?" Pay attention to your reactions. Are the sentiments you expressed Goblinspeak? Do they contradict what you've learned? Are they empty echoes, or do they have power over you when you read them? Do they send you to a landscape where you still have lessons to learn?

If so, what is this landscape? What might its lesson be? Remember, the lesson of a landscape is always empowering. It never evokes fear, sadness, anger, cynicism, or resignation. The treasure held by the Spirit of Place is meant to lead you into peace and wisdom. Do you need to take more time exploring this landscape to discover what you must learn? Are you willing to do that, now that you know you have a compass that points to true north, and allies willing to help you?

If you've discovered that the words in the Canyon of Echoes no longer ring true for you or send you back to a painful and traumatizing landscape, sit for a moment and feel your courage as your wisdom arises within you. Write down the lessons you've learned that are encapsulated in your talisman.

Choose your words carefully. Which ones do you need to start saying so that they can begin to sink into your heart?

For example:

> *I love and approve of myself. I am always safe and secure. My body is beautiful. Miracles happen without my knowing how. Spirit is the source of my supply. I trust that I will only be given what I can handle on any particular day. I am a success! I am worthy. Whatever is taken from me will be replaced by something better. Spirit knows the form that is best for me* [and so on].

(I have a special book where I've collected my favorite affirmations over the years, and especially lately, I open it up daily and say these empowering words out loud! My dogs and plants are very happy because of it, I'm sure.)

Return your awareness to the Crystal Canyon of Echoes where you are standing. Look to your side. There is the Gentle Gardener, holding a basket of seedpods with wispy wings. All around you, you notice that your affirmations have bounced off the walls of the Crystal Canyon of Echoes and become seeds floating in the air. The Gentle Gardener is gathering every one of them for you. Are you ready to plant them? Describe what will grow if you choose to plant these seeds.

I suggest that in one month, you return to what you've written in your journal as a result of this exercise, reread it, and ask yourself, "Are these words true for me now? Do they generate emotions in me, or are they discarded beliefs that don't affect me anymore?" Repeat this process once a month for a year, each time journaling about the progress you've made in letting go of old beliefs that aren't serving you and embracing new ones that give you courage, joy, and a greater sense of self-worth.

The Reality of Magic

You'd think that if we could agree on one thing, it's what reality is. I'm sure we'd all be comfortable saying that yes, we share the same planet with other human beings—as well as common basic biological needs and attributes—and we all know perfectly well that the sun will rise in the east and set in the west.

But researchers on the frontiers of science have a new picture of reality that tells us that the concrete, material world isn't solid after all; rather, it's a "holographic blur" of frequencies, as author Michael Talbot describes it in his book *The Holographic Universe*. Some scientists have recently discovered that as little as 3 percent of what we experience as physical reality is solid, made up of matter. Meanwhile, 97 percent is an unknown invisible power that keeps the smallest bits of "stuff," or physical reality, buzzing around in a quantum space, creating the illusion that we're looking at a solid object rather than a dense cloud.

At the tiniest level of reality, particles of "stuff" become waves of light, and vice versa, simply by being observed. With this knowledge, we can start to understand that our shared reality is a product of perception. When we change the way we view our experiences, the world responds accordingly.

When you get right down to it, physical reality is an illusion of perception. At the quantum level, a human being consists of a bunch of lights turning on and off, storing, sending, and receiving information encoded into energy. When you open your brain, you don't see a sunset there. However, you've *experienced* a sunset and can recognize a new one, so at the level of energy or consciousness, that sunset exists as a memory or a thought, even though it's not a physical reality right now.

Where does the reality of thought "live"? Not in my dog's brain, that's for certain. He's not thinking about whether I'm going to buy a new bag of treats for him this weekend, or pondering what it felt like to go "walkies" yesterday. His consciousness is totally focused on the now, and he has only the vaguest sense of what came before and what might come later: he'll wag his tail when I grab his leash, and cower when the groomer comes over.

In contrast, we humans can use our minds to create or re-create experiences that are completely out of sync with the physical reality we're in at the moment. If I think about something terrible that happened long ago, I cry real tears. I get excited anticipating what it will be like to lead my next seminar and witness someone having a breakthrough, and can feel myself get "pumped" as adrenaline rushes through me as I think about it. None of these experiences I'm having is real in the present, just in my mind. Yet my brain registers the experience as if I were standing in front of a client in the middle of a *Shazam!* moment right now.

Here's the thing about brains: They can be very confused about the nature of reality. You can trick them fairly easily. This is why guided visualizations in which you imagine yourself smoothly navigating future challenges are so effective at enhancing performance. Your imagination becomes a magical tool because you can use it to get your brain to create a reality that, once etched in your gray matter, becomes a familiar experience you can draw upon next week when you sit down for the actual job interview or first date.

The ancients knew that we can shape reality by using our consciousness, and described this world we experience through our senses as *maya*—illusion—or a dream. Our lives are surely lived mostly through our personal perceptions created by our conscious minds and our personal and collective "unconscious." When we decide to interact with these magical realms that our minds can create, they become real for us, because we infuse them with the power of our thoughts, beliefs, and feelings.

Lynne McTaggart and Gary Schwartz, Ph.D., researchers in the field of consciousness and intention, did a blind study in which two leaves were placed next to each other in a room in Arizona. A London group led by McTaggart sent healing intention to one of the leaves. In Arizona, Schwartz was unaware of which leaf was prayed for, and measured the biophoton emissions of each, as revealed by a highly sensitive piece of equipment called a CCD camera. When the results were examined, it turned out that the one that was sent "good vibrations" had measurably stronger biophoton emissions. You may have experienced a similar transference of energy, picking up on knowledge that wouldn't be accessible to you in the ordinary reality of the senses.

Information energy travels in ways we don't understand, affecting energy fields of beings far away. My half brother, whom I'd met only twice in my life, was living in Europe when my sister, mother, and I heard from relatives that he'd suffered a massive heart attack the very hour my father had died. He hadn't communicated with my father in 25 years, yet they were entangled at the level of consciousness across great distances.

This was no coincidence. These aren't unusual experiences. To our detriment, we've been taught to ignore or dismiss such "coincidences" as meaningless.

Synchronicity holds within it the magic of awareness and connection, a magic we can work with to transform our lives. Then, too, through prayer, meditation, affirmations, visualizations, and similar techniques for altering consciousness and the energy that we send forth and receive, we can make magic. We have the ability to direct our imagination consciously. When we do, we become even more aware of the meaningful coincidences in our lives. We can have a clearer sense of the invisible forces that shape our world.

How Magic Works

To bring about the results we desire, we must *be* the reality we seek—that is, live it as if it were real, then experience it as our truth regardless of our circumstances in the external world. Then we must be open to how Spirit responds to our vibration.

Remember, Spirit is a creative force and may think up something far better than the life you'd envisioned for yourself. The real gift may lie in what you discover as you search for the object of your desire, which is why our blessings, opportunities, and gifts rarely show up where, when, and how we expect them to. When they do, it's truly a miracle, but when Spirit comes up with a more ingenious plan, it's equally miraculous.

You may indeed attract things and create a bountiful life for yourself, but you can do much better than simply manifesting material wealth and comfort. The "inside job" of self-healing and change has remarkable outer ramifications that will fulfill you more deeply than will the symbols of power and success.

We don't think of "magic" as internal alchemy, however, because we were taught to believe that it's the stuff of fairy tales and childish stories. Genuine magic doesn't work like Santa Claus: there is no "naughty and nice" list, no "If you're good, you get a prize; and if you're bad, you get nothing."

The magic of the co-creative partnership between you and Spirit isn't reduced to such a simple equation. You direct Spirit in a more subtle way by changing within. The "naughty" behavior that stems from insecurity will only be healed if you face your distorted beliefs about yourself and find compassion for who you are. All-knowing, all-loving Spirit is far more interested in granting you the gift of self-love than in something so simplistic as punishing you for acting badly out of fear and self-hatred. You'll experience the consequences that push you to grow, because that's what the Divine wants for you. Surrender to this awesome experience of real magic and marvel at the mystery of how Spirit will always find a way to lead you toward the healing path.

The wand is yours to take up; the stream of consciousness that is both infinite and rich with creativity is waiting for you to connect with it. Sit in the chair of the Wizard of Awareness and begin the art of making magic in your life.

Traveler's Notes

- There is a nonlocal reality that we call magic. We interact with this reality on the Map, and cledons and synchronicities are evidence of this interaction.

- A cledon is an everyday sound or sight that our intuition tells us holds great meaning. It is a sign from Spirit.

- Synchronicity is a reminder from Spirit that we are all connected, all affecting each other. It reminds us that magic is at work and that we can work with the magic.

- When we pay attention to the cledons, synchronicities, and coincidences, we receive wisdom that was previously hidden to us, which can help us avoid unnecessary trips to distressing landscapes.

- Magic opens doors of opportunity that allow us to find what we are looking for, even though sometimes what we find takes a very different form than what we expected.

- The Crystal Canyon of Echoes is where we go to release the emotional resonance of old, disempowering beliefs and replace them with more empowering ones. We can go there at any time to heal our old patterns.

- Physical reality is the result of our perception. Our ability to change our perception is like a magician's wand because it allows us to shift our *reality.*

- We can work with our imagination to alter ourselves and our lives. This is the magic of our own consciousness and the power of the mind.

- Spirit wants us to heal and to feel self-love. Spirit doesn't punish or reward; it teaches, with love and compassion.

Part IV

MAKING THE MAGIC REAL

Chapter Eleven

TRAVELING COMPANIONS

*"The meeting of two personalities is like
the contact of two chemical substances: if there
is any reaction, both are transformed."*

— CARL JUNG

*"I . . . have a superstition that has grown on me as
a result of invisible hands coming all the time—namely,
that if you do follow your bliss you put yourself on a kind
of track that has been there all the while, waiting for you,
and the life that you ought to be living is the one you are
living. When you can see that, you begin to meet people who
are in the field of your bliss, and they open the doors to you.
I say, follow your bliss and don't be afraid, and doors will
open where you didn't know they were going to be."*

— JOSEPH CAMPBELL

As we journey forth on the Map, we are never alone. We have our magical allies and challengers, of course, but we also come across other travelers who will join us for part of our adventure. We're meant to learn from them and respond to their invitations for growth and healing.

Spirit picks just the right traveling companions for you. I know that it doesn't always feel that way—particularly when you think that your co-worker is going to drive you crazy, or are convinced that your neighbor is nuts and out to make your life miserable— but it's true. Your discomfort with another person is intended to make you look closer at why that individual is in your life.

The people you're meant to encounter will meet up with you on the road, unless you decide to interact with your Map in such a way as to alter your course. Only when you change the Map do you change the roster of travelers who will cross your path.

When I opened myself up to a new career, the perfect catalysts for change began to show up in my life, sometimes in the most peculiar ways. They appeared in the seat next to me on an airplane, or driving a hotel limousine (which I wrote about at length in my first book, *Remembering the Future*).

However, I've also met people who have created difficulties for me. These fellow travelers were meant to interact with me and wake me up to the choices I was making. Seen in this light, no one was to blame, and everyone was at the perfect place on my path. For every client I've read over the past 20-plus years, this is true, too: The "wrong man" is the right one for the lesson to be learned; the "wrong situation" is the classroom you were meant to be in. There is always a gift in the chaos and discord.

"Why Is This Person in My Life?"

Many people believe that the Law of Attraction says that if someone shows up in their lives, it's because they attracted that person. I know that when I'm in a lousy mood and I get into my car, it sure seems that every bad driver and tailgater in the vicinity is in my lane. I'm irritated, they're aggressive, and we are all resonating together. If you could "hear" our vibration, it would sound like a head-banging, heavy-metal rock song called "Get Out of My Way, Dammit!"

But on that same road there are drivers who are tuned in to a different frequency. They've got "Take It Easy" playing on the car stereo. They're smiling as all the angry drivers zip through the lanes and wear out their accelerators. These travelers let the others pass and give them no energy or attention.

The Law of Attraction has been misinterpreted by some to mean that we are actually acting as magnets, drawing in and repelling people and situations that perfectly match up with our vibration. This is a mechanistic view of how attraction and resonance works.

Like attracts like, so you *will* notice, approach, and interact with those you feel a connection to. However, you're not personally responsible for everyone who is on the freeway today just because you chose to go for a drive. You, like everyone else, will always be surrounded by people who are angry and intense, and others who are calmly enjoying the ride. The Law of Attraction simply ensures that you'll *notice* those vibrating at your level and overlook everyone else. So which song are you going to tune in to?

Changing the Map and Your Companions on the Road

Change your vibration, change yourself, change your enchanted Map: this is the way you change the world around you.

Because we are all interconnected, the alignment of all the Maps changes when one is redrawn. Have you ever looked through a kaleidoscope? Twist the canister ever so slightly and it realigns to a completely different pattern. The Map works similarly.

You can also think of everyone's maps intersecting like those clear plastic sheets they had in encyclopedias years ago that showed the skeleton, then the organs superimposed upon the picture, then the circulatory system overlaying that. Your map has many layers, and sometimes you puzzle over the experiences you've had and the people you've encountered because you can't see all the layers. You wonder, "What on earth was *that* experience about?" If you alter your vibration, you shift one of those clear overlays. Then everything looks different because you're no longer aligned with the other maps. The people who matched up with you and were headed your way are now going in a completely different direction from yours.

After I stopped drinking, bar culture held no attraction for me. I resisted the idea of socializing with industry insiders in places that held so many negative memories and temptations. Although the lighting in those smoky clubs didn't change, what I saw there did. I could witness the wounded egos acting out, the subtle manipulative behavior people used on others, and the lies they told themselves and started to believe after they'd had a few.

I stopped ending up in these sorts of places, and I stopped meeting the sort of people who wanted to spend all their time in bars. That's not to say that every person in a nightclub was an alcoholic in denial, or emotionally stuck in adolescence, but rather that it was a lot easier for me to avoid those types of people when I stopped hanging out at their watering holes. And, after all, if you sit in a barber shop long enough, you're going to end up with a haircut!

Today, if I were to go to a club to see a band, I'd notice the person who is glowing with enjoyment as he listens to the music and vibrates along with it, instead of being aware of those who are hiding from their feelings with a bottle of beer. My map is altered, and what I see and whom I meet has altered as well.

Although we are powerful alchemists, we never work alone. Co-creation is a group effort. Every nightclub has barflies, bands, couples on dates, fans of the musicians, and friends who congregate after a long week at work. They all create the place and the situation. Which person do you gravitate toward? And what will you co-create with that individual? How will you interact with him or her?

Sometimes we're so compelled to create a situation that if there's someone within a 100-mile radius who can help us do so, we'll find him like a bee finds the perfect flower. When I was drinking and getting high, believe me, I could find whatever drug I wanted, and the dealers could spot me a mile away. I also had a nose for abusive men that couldn't be matched. If there was one guy at a party who treated women horribly, who would be unfaithful or dishonest, I'd literally bump into him and feel an instant attraction. What we created seemed magical to me at the time because I was in a haze of alcohol and infatuation, but our "chemistry" was simply dysfunction, and what we created together was as predictable as you can imagine.

The magic of creating something new doesn't require you to change everyone and everything around you to match up with your vision of the world. The people you need to help you co-create what you desire will be there once you focus your intention and align your vibration with your highest desires, rather than tuning in to the Goblin's radio broadcast.

Your head and heart may wish for a healthy relationship that feels like a delightful haven, but you can't manifest that when you're tuned to Goblin Radio 95: "All Goblinspeak, All the Time." You know that station. You fall asleep to it, and it invades your consciousness while you sleep your way through your life. So wake up and turn down the volume on those incessant disempowering messages. That's when you'll really start creating something magical and drawing in the companions who can help you.

Some of these individuals will be in your life for a long time, others for only a few moments. Some will be allies and some will be challengers. And a few will be Magical Map Shifters.

Magical Map Shifters

The most significant traveling companions are Magical Map Shifters. They actually turn your map, realigning it and changing your path. You may then find yourself walking along a pretty country road strewn with flowers that leads to the Resting Tree, Easy Street, or the Tranquil Lake; or you could end up trudging along a muddy walkway to the Raging River or Storm Fields. My Magical Map Shifters list includes my husband, who taught me that I'm capable of having a healthy relationship with a man, but it also includes a drug dealer who led me to Rock Bottom.

Whenever you meet a Magical Map Shifter, you know that it's an unusual moment. Your senses sharpen, and you might even feel or hear the buzzing of your mutual resonance. In that moment when you meet, it's as if time stands still; the frame freezes; and you become hyperaware of what you're hearing, seeing, and experiencing.

I could tell you in detail the moment I met my husband . . . and the moment I met that drug dealer. At those fateful points, where our Maps intersected, I knew I was experiencing something profound. I was meeting the person I was meant to meet. All roads would have taken me to that spot—even though one was a meeting place of two lovers who bring each other joy, and the other was a meeting place of dysfunction and destruction. I'm sure there's someone you could name instantly whom you became acquainted with in a moment that seemed fated.

Perhaps someone else connected you with this Magical Map Shifter, saying, "I have a feeling you're going to hit it off with this person," or "There's someone I really think you should meet." Others can actually pick up on the power of your vibration and the other person's and see that you're meant to get together in some capacity. Then, when you meet the individual in question, if he truly is a Magical Map Shifter for you, you'll sense it.

A Magical Map Shifter who is an ally may be in your life for only a short time. You might have had a friend who was just the person you needed to support you during a crisis, and your involvement was emotionally intimate—even intense—but somehow the two of you parted ways. You can't even recall why you lost track of each other.

This happens because some people aren't meant to be with you for your entire journey. I'm always grateful for the blessing of interludes I've shared with wonderful people who then moved on to wherever they were meant to go.

Because Magical Map Shifters have a profound effect on you, you often tend to want to cling to them rather than move forward. Or you might simply have that person's memory close to your heart in gratitude for the impact he or she had on your life.

Then, too, if you were a Magical Map Shifter for someone, you might not realize it. That person may have been thinking about you for years, wanting to tell you how much of an effect you had on him or her.

Take my friend Jane. A woman who went to grade school and high school with Jane's mother, Noreen, 60 years prior but wasn't a close friend, showed up at her mom's funeral. She told everyone that Noreen had been the one person who gave her courage when she was bullied as a child. She'd been wanting to thank her for years and finally shared how much it had meant. For Jane, this was a magical moment, for she was gifted with a beautiful story about her mom that she'd never heard before.

I think there are a lot of secrets like that out there. Maybe over the years this woman was too embarrassed to express her gratitude to Jane's mom, but she felt a strong need to share this story with people.

I received a letter from a client whom I'd read for only once years ago thanking me for what I'd said. At the time, she had been terribly depressed about her life and had considered suicide. Because I shared the details of what happened to me, and the difficulties I had overcome, I'd given her hope. She'd wanted to thank me for years but didn't have the courage. I didn't even remember her, yet when I heard that I'd had such a powerful impact on this person, it meant the world to me. You never know how you'll touch another.

Questionable Connections

Sometimes people don't move on from those long-ago moments. My friend Marni heard from a man she dated in high school. She was the first person who believed in his musicianship, and he'd carried a torch for her for 30 years. He never fully pursued music and was at a point in his life where he wanted to begin again. He contacted my friend with a long, detailed, obsessive account of his feelings for her.

Marni was shocked and frightened that someone she only vaguely remembered had never let go of his memory of their short-lived dating experience. He had wandered the Ghostlands while she had been on her own adventure for many years. They had nothing in common, not even their memories, for she remembered their brief connection differently, and with much less emotional "charge." He projected so much onto it that he created an entire epic about it and actually became quite hostile when she rebuffed his attempt to reconnect.

Thanks to social-networking sites and the Internet, it's easier than ever for people who are wandering in the Ghostlands of nostalgia to get in touch with those they miss. While it can be wonderful to reconnect with a Magical Map Shifter, it's not a good idea to try to re-create the magic once the moment has passed. We are meant to meet, connect, and move on—not to hold on to the past with a death grip.

You might also find it enjoyable to reconnect with those you've lost track of, reminisce a bit, and go back to your life; and sometimes you'll even find you have more in common now than you did back then. Yet these reconnections don't always work out very well. Again, the past isn't always meant to be revisited. And if this person wants to take a trip down Nostalgia Lane to escape her present emotions, she can end up in a Ghostland instead of moving forward into something real. If you feel a powerful need to rekindle a relationship or friendship from the past, know that a Goblin may be pulling you toward a Ghostland, so be alert.

The best way to deal with a desire to reconnect with one of your Magical Map Shifters is to be grateful for the blessings of former times, and trust that you can create all the positive experiences and emotions you'd like today or in the future. Yet it doesn't have to be with this same person. Someone who was once hugely impactful in your life may not be in that same place again. And if someone tries to pull you back into a relationship you no longer wish to be in, don't feel guilty and get sucked into Shouldville or the Raging River.

Shouldville

Shouldville is a land of sticky social obligations. You walk down the street in your pajamas and feel exposed as people shout to you from all the open windows and doors. "Yoo-hoo!" they cry. "Come in! I have *sooooo* much to tell you." People are eager to catch you up on their dramas, and there are theaters everywhere. Goblins are like carnival barkers, trying to draw you into the matinees and make you feel guilty for losing touch with the residents of Shouldville.

You feel increasingly torn as people make demands on you, until you pull out your compass, take a seat in the chair of the Wizard of Awareness, close your eyes, and hear the Spirit of Place telling you that it's okay to have healthy boundaries. You open your eyes and see a little cottage with a fence and a wooden door. The difference between privacy and isolation is clear.

The Raging River and the Wobbly Bridge

While guilt can take you to Shouldville, a desire to fix someone else's life can land you on the banks of the Raging River. There, the rushing waters create so much noise that when you call across to the other bank—where the person you care about is suffering all alone—you find that your friend can't hear you. There is a Wobbly Bridge over this river, made of rope and a few rotting boards. This bridge is fashioned from frayed threads masquerading as strong ones; they're created by an unhealthy enmeshment, where boundaries are blurry, which weakens the true connection between you and the other person. Do you dare cross this bridge and run the risk that you'll fall into the river and be swept downstream by the heavy current?

The wisdom lesson at the Raging River and Wobbly Bridge is that it's not your job to save or fix anyone else. You can't be this person's caretaker and get him to hear you, because he is on his own map. Something in him has to change for your paths to re-align, for a new bridge to appear—it may be one that magically constructs itself when his inner landscape changes, or it may be one he chooses to build because he wants to accept your help.

Many of us try to defy the nature of the Raging River and the Wobbly Bridge because it's painful to watch someone we love suffer. The following exercise can help you avoid getting stuck in this problematic landscape.

Exercise: The Raging River and the Wobbly Bridge

In your journal, write an account of a person in your life whom you've tried your best to help, rescue, or change for the better. What disastrous decisions did this person make? How did you try to lend assistance?

When you've recounted your tale, envision yourself on the banks of a raging river of white-water rapids. The person you love is on the other bank, unable to see or hear you.

Look around you. Is there a bridge nearby? How far across it can you get before you must stop, for your own safety?

Begin to cross the bridge. Stop when you feel it's too dangerous to go on.

At your feet is a board with a message written on it. Look down and read it. What does it say? How do you feel when you read this message?

Remember that your compass can summon your magical allies to help you at this point. What will you do now?

What are your allies whispering to you? Are they reminding you of your talisman, of the lesson you've learned from having been here before, now encapsulated in this magical tool that provides you with the courage to change your course and leave this landscape behind you?

Close your eyes and have faith. Feel compassion for yourself, for the other person, for all people and all creatures.

Take the next step, the one you know is right for you.

Where are you?

Empathy, Courage, and the Sharing of Stories

The quality of empathy requires you to understand your own emotional states well enough to recognize them in other people. You can't advise someone if you have no awareness of the features of his or her inner landscape. But if you've been there and you have a talisman, you can be of great help to others . . . and they can help *you*, sometimes in unexpected ways. When you give, you might be surprised by what you receive.

Empathy allows you to build a bridge, but you don't have to go dashing over it to rescue the other person. Simply by building it, you can help someone find the wisdom of the landscape she feels trapped in. Your love may awaken in her the courage to stop panicking and locate her compass.

Your empathy also has the power to rouse people in the Field of Poppies, but remember that everyone has an enchanted Map that is in constant motion, aligning and going out of alignment with other maps. You can't always "awaken" people; they may not hear you when you offer wisdom. Let go of the outcome. Speak the truth in love and you might be surprised by who else hears your call.

As I mentioned in the last chapter, when I speak in front of hundreds of people (or to the thousands of listeners on my weekly radio show), I tell my audience to pay close attention because while a message I deliver may not seem to be for them, it might actually contain the very wisdom they need to hear. We share so many human experiences, yet we convince ourselves that "no one could possibly understand" what we're going through.

187

The success rate is high in 12-step programs because people who share the same experiences come together to heal. In AA, for example, most of the alcoholics attending know what it's like to experience the hell of low self-worth and shame. But there are members who have moved past that, and revealing their experiences of strength and hope brings about an air of magic and power. Coming together to share helps new members find the courage to change and heal. These programs are metaphysical in nature, as the group truly initiates miracles in people's lives. The AA saying "No matter how far down the scale you've gone, you can see how your experience can benefit others" reminds us that our life experiences can be a powerful talisman for someone else.

These 12-step programs for people with addictive behaviors are extremely effective in part because they thrive on community, on gathering wisdom and courage and channeling it to everyone in the room, even the person sitting in the last chair in the back who isn't sure he belongs there. It's a place where people are nourished and supported, and invited to bring their shadow into the light for healing. The AA slogan "You are no longer alone" is one that we would all be wise to adopt, given that isolation and separation are the root causes of our feelings of alienation.

You don't need to be an addict or alcoholic to benefit from such a community. You just need to reach out; and if there are no such groups available, start one with others who want to share wisdom, courage, love, and support. Your intention alone will shift your Map to intersect with others of like mind and vibration.

Remember how I said that all talismans are connected at a quantum level, at the level of light, energy, and information? *Your* courage grows when you connect with others' courage through the sharing of stories.

When I do online courses, I have a forum where participants can actively take part in a dialogue of support with each other. Even though they're in different cities, or even different countries, and may not seem to have a lot of similarities on the surface, people find common ground and share their courage and vulnerability. The level of support strangers can give each other is inspiring.

If you don't feel supported in your journey, remember that the people you're seeking with an open heart are there. You just need to open up to them. The Maps will shift; an intersection point will occur; and you can have an extraordinary exchange of love, empathy, and courage.

Sharing stories is talismanic work. It helps you realize that you're not living on an island but on a "sandbar of me," and you have the ability to part the waters and see the connections you share with others, connections that lie underneath the illusion of separateness.

We share a collective consciousness and experience. Tap into it and the Magical Map Shifters become obvious to you. They are everywhere.

Courageous Connections

Although we seek intimacy and security, our fears cause us to try to control exactly how our interactions with fellow travelers play out. It takes guts to face an adversary and respond not with a battle cry but with love and compassion for both ourselves and that person.

Looking within at your own wound will make you feel vulnerable and unsafe. It's also the only way to find your courage. Courage isn't the absence of fear. It's feeling the fear and stepping forward anyway.

If you don't have a talisman to help you hold your ground and make a clear decision about what to do next, you need to explore your inner landscape. The harsh light that the Gentle Gardener or the Bone Collector sheds on the land, exposing what you've denied, isn't easy to tolerate. If you're willing to do it, however, you'll realize that although the intensity may initially hurt your eyes, it is a healing light.

What can it heal within you? What do you need to acknowledge so that you can let it go, or claim it as yours? What weeds do you need to pull? What flowers do you need to plant? Traveling companions, whether they are allies or adversaries, can help you find the answers to these questions.

One way they do so is through the mentor-student relationship. Often, Magical Map Shifters partner with others through archetypal relationships that appear to be one-sided, as if one person is giving and the other receiving, when in actuality, both people are benefiting.

Once we graduate from school, most of us don't look for teachers, yet the mentor-student relationship is a powerfully transformative dynamic two people can share. A student can learn from one who has been there, who already has a talisman and knows the secret of the landscape. However, the student has to have an open heart in order to experience that wisdom and use it. And while a mentor gives to her student, she also receives. In teaching, we learn something about ourselves and gain insights we might never have had if we hadn't tried to guide someone else.

All the great adventure stories have teachers and students: Yoda and Luke Skywalker. Dumbledore and Harry Potter. Gandalf and Frodo. As grand and brilliant as the mentor may be, however, eventually the student enlightens *him*. The teacher needs to remember that there is always something to be learned, and that the process of instructing others yields the opportunity to learn even more. The trick is to continue to grow in wisdom but not lock ourselves into the egotistical belief that we are experts who should never be questioned.

If you're not careful, the Goblin will drive you to the base of Mount Hubris, a foolish little dunghill that thinks it is a mighty mountain. The only way to get past this smelly heap is to cut through the manure. It is not a pleasant experience!

Be a humble mentor, and *find* one who isn't too enamored of himself and his expertise. Mentors are often elders, but not always. They're usually more experienced than the student in some way. A coach, leader, or therapist may be much younger than you are yet offer brilliant insights and guidance to you in a certain area of your life. Someone who has come through the same experience—divorce, cancer, loss of a child, caretaking for an ailing parent—can be your mentor as well.

Because we all long for a sense of purpose, many people set themselves up as mentors when they lack the wisdom they hope to impart. Always have your eyes open to the fact that mentors can be more wounded than they let on. Those you wish to emulate are the ones who may surprise you with their humanity. Don't place people on a pedestal. They will surely fall off.

I have a favorite author whose words have changed my life, yet this person isn't very kind when you meet him face-to-face, one-on-one. I know that the message is much more important than the messenger, though. I always say: take what you like, what resonates, and leave the rest, with compassion for the messenger.

No one is perfect. We are all works in progress. All of us are teaching tools for others.

Traveler's Notes

- Every Map intersects with all others, and on it are traveling companions whose paths intersect with ours.

- When we alter our Map, the intersection points change. We end up changing the roster of people we will meet.

- Traveling companions are often meant to teach us valuable lessons.

- Your discomfort with another person is meant to make you look closer at why that individual is in your life.

- The Law of Attraction ensures that you'll notice those who are vibrating at your level and overlook everyone else.

- The most significant companions are Magical Map Shifters. Whether they serve as allies or challengers, and regardless of how long they're in your life, they have a profound effect on you.

- You can feel that it is a special moment when you meet someone who will serve as a Magical Map Shifter for you.

- If you have an opportunity to reconnect with a Magical Map Shifter from your past, don't attempt to re-create the special moment that has already passed.

- If you try to relive the magic that you once shared with the Magical Map Shifter, you may end up in a Ghostland of nostalgia. If that person pressures you to relive the magic, you may end up feeling you are in Shouldville, the land of obligations.

- You can't be responsible for another person's journey. If you try to rescue that individual or fix her life, you end up at the Raging River, with its Wobbly Bridge.

- Treasure the blessing of the Magical Map Shifters in your life, and the privilege of having had the opportunity to be one for someone else.

~ Chapter Twelve ~

WHERE WILL YOU GO FROM HERE?

"Participate joyfully in the sorrows of the world. We cannot cure the world of sorrows but we can live in joy. When the world seems to be falling apart the rule is to hang on to your bliss."

— JOSEPH CAMPBELL

"Only by much searching and mining, are gold and diamonds obtained, and man can find every truth connected with his being, if he will dig deep into the mine of his soul."

— JAMES ALLEN

Follow your own inner guidance and your heart's desires. If your compass is pointed to Spirit, you'll be shown the way. Even if you're unclear about where you're going to end up, being immersed in the adventure is the point. Once you get the hang of how your Map works, you can't help but see the signs that will guide you. Your experience is always your own even though it's connected to others'. This is the truth about being *in* the world but not *of* it. You choose your routes in conjunction with your most important traveling companion and the co-creator of your Map: Spirit. What does your journey look like now?

> *You emerge on the other side of the Immovable Mountain only to see a large hand-lettered sign that warns:* BEWARE OF THE DRAGON AHEAD.
>
> *Your companion says, "Oh, I don't believe in dragons. I say affirmations daily, you know, and I focus my intent on achieving abundance and joy. So there can't possibly be a dragon up the road."*
>
> *Much as you would like to believe that positive thinking will protect you from all manner of "dragons," you are torn. Experience has shown you that you can get burned, that your map has some parameters you can't change. You have come to accept these limitations, and learned to walk between the pillar of acceptance and that of co-creation. You are a responsible and discerning mapmaker who has no interest in a side trip to smelly Mount Hubris, the place we go when we overestimate our power to determine all the details of our journey.*
>
> *"I think I'll try to find another route," you say.*
>
> *"But time is short!" cries your companion. "You might be on a detour forever, just because you're afraid of some silly story about a dragon."*
>
> *You smile. "There are no detours," you say. "The path I'm about to take must be the one I was <u>meant</u> to take."*
>
> *"And which path is that?" asks your companion.*
>
> *"I don't know. But it will show itself to me if I'm patient. That much I know."*

Now that you've learned the art of being your own cartographer, you'll feel that your interactions with your Map are much more within your control even as you experience a greater sense of surrender to Spirit. The bottom line is that you have the choice to turn fate into destiny when your bliss, which is an expression of your higher nature, is what propels you forward. You're aware now that you can fire the transportation director who booked you on a train to the Storm Fields, or jostled you mercilessly on a dilapidated bus before dumping you in the Sticky Swamp. You've learned how to lull your inner Goblin to sleep so you're no longer tricked by his disempowering messages.

Now you're able to *anticipate* changes. You'll feel the rumbling underneath your feet, notice the sudden drop in temperature as the clouds block the sun, and recognize that you're about to be pulled into a new environment. One phone call or one remark can trigger an emotional reaction, but you'll find that it's less intense, and arises more slowly, giving you time to notice that you're uncomfortable and your Goblin is stirring. Now you know that you don't have to let your emotions sweep you up and take you someplace you'd prefer not to go, because you have the ability to sit in the seat of the Wizard of Awareness, take up your wand, and begin to interact with your map in a more satisfying way.

You also now have a hard-earned talisman that crystallizes the wisdom you've acquired. You won't have to "go there" when you encounter someone who speaks abusively to you and expects you to engage in the kind of drama that you know will only land you in Flatville, where all stories lack nuance and everyone identifies with being a victim. Instead, you can place your hand around this beautiful gem that is yours because you've earned it. You can feel its warm glow. Courage, love, compassion, and faith will be kindled in you, because this magical talisman's energy is connected to all the other talismans out there, created by all the other heroes who bravely faced the challenges of the land and internalized its wisdom.

Your talisman will give you the courage to disengage from situations that will tickle your Goblin and cause him to spring to life. You'll be able to walk away, or face the challenges you can't avoid.

What you may not realize is that you can also harness the energy of the Goblin. Energy can't be created or destroyed, but it can be used as fuel, so when the Goblin is sleeping, you'll have access to more energy to sustain your courage to change and become the person who lives the life you dream of. When you cease listening to the Goblin's frantic urgings that compel you to look for power outside of yourself in money and influence—when you stop trying to control all the details of your life—you'll find your genuine power. It lies in being willing to learn and to acquire wisdom as you open yourself up to the unknown and to the will of Spirit, the Divine cartographer who set the boundaries and parameters of your map.

Deciding on Your Destination

Once you've claimed your mapmaking power, the question is whether to remain in your current landscape or go someplace else—and if you go, what should be your destination? You may be unsure of the path to take, and hesitate even as the ground underneath you is shifting.

Perhaps you must go to the place we all enter when we're ambivalent and need to sort through our mixed emotions and confusing thoughts so that our intuition can tell us which path to travel next. . . .

Feeling Ambivalent in the Corridor of Uncertainty

Karen Armstrong, in her book *The Case for God,* talks about a "strident lust for certainty" that we all share despite the fact that unknowing is built into the human condition and something we must acknowledge. Even after doing readings and accurately predicting the future for many people, I'm aware that the power isn't in knowing what the days ahead are likely to hold, but in greeting the uncertainty with a sense of wonder, awe, and patience—all of which open the door to clarity.

In the Corridor of Uncertainty, you may feel pressed for time, but to rush through the first door you find unlocked is a mistake.

If you do, you're likely to end up in a rebound relationship, or a job that wasn't anything like you thought it would be. The lesson here is provided by the Wizard of Awareness, who moves slowly and mindfully and beckons you to do the same.

You climb into his chair and find that you have the time to look closely at what's around you. You ask yourself, "Does this activity or relationship have value for me? Why am I doing this? Why have I made the decisions I've made, and are they still working for me?" You slow down and ponder the insights that come to you as you hold your wand so that it taps into the stream of consciousness, where information hidden from your conscious mind can be accessed.

When you stop to consider why you're here, how you got here, and where you might want to go, you soon find that you're experiencing clarity. Your intent becomes known to you, and in an instant, it becomes known to the universe as well. In that magical moment, the universe begins to align with your intent. You hear the clicking of locks that disengage and know that many of the doors lining this long Corridor of Uncertainty are open to you. But which do you choose?

Because you've set aside your confusion, frustration, and impatience, the answer becomes clear to you. You know that while the door you choose may not immediately lead you to a landscape you find pleasant, it is nevertheless the right one. If you step through the doorway and discover that the road you begin to travel twists and turns unexpectedly, it's not because you've been forced to take a detour, but because this is how adventurous journeys unfold. You can't always understand why you end up on a certain road until much later, when you look back and can see how it led to where you were supposed to be.

Remember that the voice of your intuition, which points out the door to choose, can always be trusted, and you can distinguish it from the voice of the trickster Goblin by its quality. If fear, anger, impulsiveness, or acquiescence color the thoughts you experience when contemplating a decision, your inner Goblin is awake and dancing wildly. Intuition speaks with calm, sure words of courage. Fortunately, you know how to quiet that rambunctious little fellow so that you may better hear the clear voice of your intuition, which is always guided by Spirit.

Making the Choice to Travel to a Distressing Landscape

As you come to embrace your role as co-creator of the Map and learn the skill of interacting with it, you may actually choose to travel to a distressing land. It's not that you *enjoy* feeling sad or angry, but rather that you know you're going to end up in that emotional landscape anyway, and you'd like to make the trip when you're fully prepared to work through your emotions.

You may also wish to visit the Valley of Loss to process your feelings about a breakup, or to the Immovable Mountain to discover how to get past something that has been blocking you for too long. Sometimes it will feel right for you to visit the Crystal Canyon of Echoes, where you won't feel the strong, harsh emotions attached to your old beliefs and you can watch them fade as you replace them with more empowering thoughts. You might also choose to travel to the Corridor of Uncertainty and experience patience as you await the inner wisdom that will guide you to the correct door. As the emotions you've been repressing and avoiding flare up, know that you'll only feel them for exactly as long as you need to.

Children are much wiser than we are when it comes to sadness, anger, or grief. They feel the emotion and move on to something more fun and interesting within minutes . . . then return to those feelings suddenly, allow them to rise and fall, and then trot off to play again.

As adults, we tend to give so much weight to our painful feelings that if they begin to subside, we'll start penning an entire novel about why we should continue to feel sad. Then we make sadness a landscape that traps us. We actually give our feelings a much longer shelf life than they need. In a way, our stories are like hydrogenated oils, preserving and sustaining our emotions far past their expiration date.

As you allow your inner awareness to guide your choices and become your own oracle, you'll start to transform yourself and your life. Some of your fellow traveling companions will resist your changes, however, and you may have to travel to the Valley of Loss to say good-bye to relationships that you valued but which can no longer be maintained.

When I was a crazy alcoholic, I had a lot of drinking buddies; and when I sobered up, they didn't like the "new" me. Even my mother had ambivalence about my sobriety. She spent a lot of time in Flatville, telling a two-dimensional story about a good mother who rescued her hapless, screwed-up daughter, dependent on these efforts to save her. As long as I was a mess, my mom knew that I would never abandon her. Her challenge was to redefine her relationship with me and trust in our connection despite the fact that I no longer needed her to bail me out of some new disaster I'd brought about.

People who are living under the influence of their own Goblins often will be very uncomfortable with your moving forward. They don't have the courage to realign their map, and when you alter yours, you may have to go in one direction as they go in another. It can be very painful to recognize that the people you care about can't support your healing and growth, but remember that new traveling companions will meet you on the road ahead. Take your time in the Valley of Loss, where you can grieve what is past.

Sometimes we hold on to our difficult emotions because, while we don't enjoy them, they're familiar, and that gives us a sense of comfort. We remain in the Valley of Loss, at the base of the Immovable Mountain, or caught in the Raging River, struggling but unwilling to leave unless it's to take a narcotic nap in the Field of Poppies. We want to believe we can move through this traumatizing place but are loath to end up in yet another harrowing landscape . . . one that doesn't feel quite so familiar but causes just as much suffering. We manage day to day, despite our unhappiness. Soon we are in Acquiescence Alley, settling for scraps we've salvaged from garbage cans.

How do we move on? In any landscape, courage is the key to escape. We find it when we let go of our expectations of how life is supposed to be and discover that without our attachments we still have the capacity to experience joy and tranquility. I was shocked by how calm I felt at Rock Bottom. There was incredible beauty in surrender to Spirit, a liberation I'd never known before.

Letting go of your beliefs about what you must have or experience in order to be joyful is possible. The following powerful exercise will show you that you have a greater capacity for surrender than you might have believed.

Exercise: The Seven Layers of Letting Go

I was introduced to a very interesting exercise that originated with Joseph Campbell in the late 1940s. He conducted it with his comparative-mythology students to challenge their issues with attachment. I adapted it and presented it for the first time to a group of 60 participants at an intensive seminar I facilitated, sponsored by Hay House, in Scottsdale, Arizona. Here's a version you can use to help yourself learn to tolerate the possibility of loss, something we must all face at some point:

1. First, set aside an evening when you can be sure that you'll remain undisturbed for a couple of hours: no phone calls, no texting. These two hours are to be spent without any outside contact or interference. Mark the date on your calendar, making it special.

2. Prepare a sacred bath that you'll take after the exercise: Throw two handfuls of sea salt and two handfuls of Epsom salts into the bathwater. Ideally, also add six drops each of lavender, orange, basil, and eucalyptus essential oils. You can find all of these items at any health-food store.

3. Place a candle in the bathroom, and be ready to light it. Also, find a large empty bowl that you can use while doing this exercise and place it near you as you sit in the bathroom.

4. Light your candle. Say this affirmation aloud: "My attachments are not the source of my supply. God is the source of my supply. I am now ready to let go. I am safe. All is well."

5. Take out a journal and pen. When you're ready to begin, ask Spirit to help you be rigorously honest and willing to follow through with what this exercise will symbolically require of you.

6. Remove seven pages from your journal, and on each one write what you feel you couldn't possibly let go of in your life. Take your time to contemplate what this means. What could you never, ever live without? Do you occasionally say, "I would rather die than be without my husband, kids, nice home, good wine, health, financial security [and so forth]"? Think about it. What is it that you would never be able to let go of and still be happy?

7. Imagine that you're walking toward a temple gleaming in the sunlight. A huge archangel stands before you. He tells you that you must give up each of these things that are deeply meaningful to you in order to reach heaven. He asks you to follow him. You walk down a long flight of steps that leads to a ledge at the edge of a cliff. He says he will fly to a certain point in a special valley: the Valley of Loss. The only way you can get to the sacred ground of heaven, and peace and wholeness, is to follow his instructions. If you don't give up all of the seven treasures you love dearly, you'll be lost here forever.

8. When you're ready, arrange the seven papers in order of ascending importance: On the top of the pile, place the page that denotes the one thing out of the seven that maybe, just maybe, you could give up. This step will take time, as you'll probably change your mind again and again before you settle on the final order. Now, number the pages.

9. Imagine that the angel brings you to the first step into the valley. You must completely let go of the first treasure that you're attached to, even though you believe you can't possibly do so and continue to live. The angel tells you that you have no choice. Spend as much time as you need to as you contemplate giving up

this loved one, place, thing, or identity. Let the ramifications of leaving it behind permeate your whole being. Allow your emotions to come to the surface. Now, place this first piece of paper into the empty bowl. Feel the sorrow of your loss.

10. Repeat this contemplation and letting-go process with each of the other six items you thought you couldn't live without, which you've recorded on pieces of paper and arranged by priority. Fully *feel* your emotions as you give up each one.

11. When the feelings of loss have subsided, picture the angel standing guard at the gate to the sacred heavenly place of peace and wholeness. Imagine him saying to you, "You are very brave. You are ready to pass through the gate and collect all that you have lost." In your mind, step through the gate.

12. Take the papers out of the bowl and hold them close to your heart. Recognize that you can have every one of these things forever, but that you may have to experience them in a different form than you're used to. All of them continue to be yours, but they don't *belong* to you anymore. Each has the essence of the Divine and will never disappear, only transform. You'll always be able to be in contact with this essence.

13. Spend a minimum of 15 minutes soaking in your bath, contemplating what it means to love and to be without attachment. You are free. Imagine just *being* with those you care about, instead of being enmeshed with them.

One of my clients wrote to tell me that when performing this ritual, she sat in the tub laughing and crying as she threw the contents of her bowl into the bath with her to signify being surrounded with what she loved, without ownership. As you perform this exercise, do whatever moves you. It's a profound way to recognize that you must let go of attachments in order to authentically inhabit your true self and "be in the world, but not of it."

Making the Choice to Travel to a Delightful Place

We also hold on to emotions when we feel guilty about being happy, or not entitled to relaxation, rest, or fun.

Feelings of loyalty to a spouse who died, or a false belief that you're lazy or undeserving, can keep you from picking up your walking stick and traveling to the Tranquil Lake; the Resting Tree; or more active, joyful locales such as the Peaks of Joy, Adventure Land, or Balancing Beach. Like all lands on the Map, these are places you are meant to experience.

Frolicking in Adventure Land

Life is an adventure; and when we feel that to be true, we're vitalized, hopeful, happy, and—if we just came through a particularly difficult time—downright joyful. In fact, some say that Adventure Land is located on the Peaks of Joy, at the borders of the lands where our suffering is the greatest.

In Adventure Land, the amusements are everywhere. You can sit and enjoy the show at the theater, indulge in a few treats, and revel in the feeling of being surrounded by happy people. There are fun rides, games of chance in which you can win a big teddy bear, and a water park where you can grab a raft and coast down a waterslide with other cheerful companions.

Then again, Adventure Land, like all landscapes, is a magical place, so it might have very different features that bring about these emotional experiences inside *you*. It is the place where you're a child again, completely engaged in the sheer pleasure of being alive.

Everyone gets to go to Adventure Land. You don't have to earn your way there, sacrifice to pay for the ticket, or wait for someone to tell you it's okay to visit this realm of ebullience. You get to go there simply because happiness and fun are part of being human, and you deserve to experience them.

Of course, you can't remain in Adventure Land forever, but it is a marvelous place to go inside your mind and heart. This is especially true when you've come from a painful landscape, whether it's the Valley of Loss or the Frozen Land, where you've numbed your feelings and waited for rejuvenation.

You reach Adventure Land when the Goblin is napping. You can go to it by making a conscious choice to experience happiness. Laughter brings you there in an instant, and so does having an impromptu party with your friends where there's no pressure to be the perfect host. You also arrive there when you share a joke with a stranger and feel a sense of connection, if only for a brief moment, as you remember that the Map is populated by many delightful people you can encounter at any time. You can also open the gates to Adventure Land while sitting in the subway or on the bus on your way to work. Look at every person you see and imagine him or her happy and beautiful. Do this for more than five minutes and you will feel that fun, playful sense of Adventure Land.

For many months, one of my clients, Janine, had been care-taking for her elderly mother, who was in very poor health, and she'd finally made the difficult decision to put her mom in full-time hospice care. Janine continued visiting her daily, but one day she realized that the summer was passing and she hadn't taken her children to the nearby water park.

Although she was very reluctant to skip visiting her mother for one day, knowing how few days her mom had left, Janine decided that her children deserved to have this adventure with her. Her kids coaxed her into taking her first ride down a colorful water-filled tunnel. As she began to slide down the chute, she felt as if she were descending a birth canal, being reborn into joy, freedom, and the carefree world of a child, if only for a few minutes. She surrendered to gravity, to the twists and turns that spilled her out into the big pool of water warmed by the sunshine.

Janine had been advised by many concerned friends to "be sure to take time" for herself, but it wasn't until she spent this day with her children that she started to understand why making a trip to Adventure Land was so important. And while she couldn't go there every day in real life, she gave herself permission to do so on her Map.

To enjoy Adventure Land, Janine had to ignore the scolding of the Goblin, who insisted that she was a bad daughter. In the days that followed, she began to be fully present with her kids instead of always preoccupied—to feel that she was entitled to let go of her grief and worry for a few minutes over dinner before she drove up to the hospice facility each night. She even allowed herself to skip a night when she was particularly tired or worn-out emotionally, and was able to do so without feeling guilty or bad about herself.

All of us have to take time for pleasure. You may need a break for quiet and restfulness, or for reconnecting with your vitality, pleasure, and hope. You can only struggle for so long before you have to find your way to the respite of a delightful landscape.

Having a Ball on Balancing Beach

While the Ruthless Balancer in the Land of Unfairness may seem like a harsh character, he can teach you a valuable lesson about balance that may lead you to the good times on Balancing Beach.

This land always has perfect weather for sunbathing and napping, for reading a good book and chatting with old friends. You can lounge; or you can get up and play in the waves, toss a beach ball around, take a boat ride, or snorkel. On Balancing Beach, you have a choice between action and rest, and feel no guilt or distress when you choose one and not the other. Whether lying down or in motion, you're at peace because you have a sense of *balance*. Whatever you're doing is the perfect choice for you right now.

Again, to experience this lovely landscape, free from difficult emotions, you have to quiet the Goblin. Listen to his rantings without believing his story of how you must do this or that; and when he gets drowsy, show him to the little cabana where he can snooze away the afternoon. Then have yourself a ball at Balancing Beach.

Delighting in the Sanctuary of Home

A conscientious traveler always knows how to find his way home and takes time to delight in its five rooms of *love, security, meaning, creativity,* and *joy.* If you're an unconscious traveler, led around by the Goblin—the self that's driven by fear and anger—you'll end up looking outside yourself for the qualities of home, for the place of belonging and safety that serves as a base for your adventures. Then you won't be a traveler so much as a hapless wanderer, and you'll always feel lost.

In your archetypal home, comfortable in your own skin, you can experience your co-creative nature flourishing. Instead of inventing avoidance behaviors that never really work to keep you out of difficult landscapes, you're able to use your creative powers to fashion the life you want for yourself. Although there are always parameters on the Map, you can experience anything you want to experience, in some form at some time. Be open-minded about the "how" of your dream's unfolding, and surrender to Spirit, who will attend to the specifics. Then you can make quantum leaps in your self-healing and personal evolution.

Too often, we mistake "familiarity" for "home" and are uncomfortable feeling loved or safe, or feeling ourselves transforming in a positive way. We have to become used to dwelling in our *real* home: the place of self-esteem, compassion, humility, and generosity, where we accept ourselves fully and therefore have the courage to evolve. It's this courage that leads us to our purpose, to our unique way of being of service to the world.

The hero returns home from his journey after he heals himself and, as a result of this inner work, brings back something that can help his entire community. He doesn't have to experience total healing, though—just enough to find the courage and wisdom that he can share with others.

All change, even when you've longed for it and worked for it, is unsettling. That's the natural consequence of the chronic human urge for certainty. However, when you're at home within yourself, you're better able to tolerate the shift and begin to accept it without wondering, *Do I really belong in this life, in this wonderful relationship, in this perfect job for me?* You start to claim your home as your own, to recognize that you belong here, in a secure place. Emotionally, you're open; your is door unlocked (but not removed from its hinges), so anyone can walk in at any time. You invite others to your table and break bread with them, as you and your company dream up some new adventures.

Because you have this safety zone of home within, you have the courage and strength that helps you when you're in the Barren Desert or Valley of Loss. Your Goblin naps often, and you're able to remember your power to consciously choose which lands you'll travel to.

Let home be your base for growth and adventure—the place where shadows exist but there is always a light on, provided by Spirit, who dwells within you. Whenever you're scared or feeling lost, grab the hand of Spirit and say, "I don't know. Please guide me!" Then relief will flood over you, because you'll know that you *will* find your way home . . . and you'll never be lost again.

After all, there's no place like home.

if i close my eyes the truth is familiar

BY NANCY LEVIN

the trick is
to find the silence
the stillness
the space between

tear away at the layers
i am a palimpsest
many lives erased
recollections seep through
what hides inside the quiet
the calm beneath the chaos

visions are often
accompanied
by murmurings
of the dead
let go
magic takes over
leaving the living
to pursue renewal

time is standing still
watching
lives on lives
beforeafter

knowing what you are
who you are
changes from moment to moment
from mind to eye to hand

the journey turned to history
most known and best loved

clarity comes from miles away
passion paints you
wraps you
awakens the imagination

truth must be discovered
moment to moment
a remembered truth
is a dead thing
it is the past

which links us
even in its absence
but it is the present
which we call our own
while the future looms
provokes and seduces

creativity from chaos
balanced around the heart
this body
is only a marker

LIST OF
MAGICAL PLACES

There are myriad lands on your Map, all of which are reflective of your inner psycho-spiritual landscape. Here are some you might visit, but I encourage you to imagine even more or to draw inspiration from movies and books that feature rich landscapes. Explore and learn!

Acquiescence Alley. You find yourself here when you settle for less than you desire or deserve because you've lost faith and hope, and feel a lack of self-worth. In Acquiescence Alley, the scarcity will drive you to dig in garbage cans for sustenance, unless you find the courage to accept and value yourself, which are the keys to escape.

Adventure Land. Usually Adventure Land is an amusement park or a water park, but it is always a place of fun and excitement. You come here to take a break from the challenges of life, but you mustn't linger and let it become a Ghostland.

Balancing Beach. On Balancing Beach, you can sunbathe and nap, frolic in the water, or take a long walk and collect seashells. Here there is a balance between rest and joyful action, and everything you do feels right: you experience no guilt or thoughts about how you should be doing something else.

The Barren Desert. In the Barren Desert, you're exhausted and feel like there is very little in the way of sustenance. It's as if nothing can grow and your supply of creativity has dried up, but you can find nourishment and vitality here in hidden places if you become resourceful.

Codependent Land. You end up in Codependent Land when you get involved with an addict or alcoholic, or you simply become so enmeshed in other people's lives that you lose your sense of independence and self-worth. In fact, in this land everything is entangled with sticky, spidery webs. Looking into the fun-house mirrors that are all over Codependent Land, you feel that if you could contort yourself "just so," everything would be okay and the other person would be healthy, happy, and responsible. You must rid yourself of this illusion and practice radical acceptance, saying, "I didn't cause it, I can't cure it, and I can't control it."

The Corridor of Uncertainty. As you walk down this long corridor, you see one door of opportunity after another, but when you try the knobs, you find that all of the doors seem to be locked. Surrender to this experience and trust that Spirit will reveal which one to open to take you exactly where you should go. The lesson is to be still and wait. When in doubt, don't.

The Crystal Canyon of Echoes. In this place of learning and growth, the crystal walls reflect not only your words, which echo about the canyon, but the image you present to the world. Work with this canyon and you can replace old beliefs that no longer serve you with new ones that empower you.

Easy Street. On Easy Street, everyone dwells in a penthouse, sleeps until noon, and can relax into a life of luxury. You have no worries or fears and can enjoy the abundance available to you at all times. Like all places that seem to offer nothing but pleasure and relaxation, Easy Street has a shadow side: there are many trapdoors here that lead to the Field of Poppies, where you're unconscious and can't enjoy life.

The Enchanted Woods. The Woodland Sprite will teach you all about the Enchanted Woods. Just like the forest in the fairy tales from childhood, the Enchanted Woods can be frightening or nurturing, depending on how you interact with them and whom you meet. That is the lesson here. You're a magical mapmaker and have the ability to zoom in and out, to change your perspective. When you can't see the forest for the trees, or the trees for the forest, you must take some time in the Enchanted Woods and learn perspective and the value of noticing the big picture *and* the details. Within these woods lies the forest grove, where the trees part and you can look up to see the open sky and recall that you're never stuck in a landscape—that there is always an escape route, even if you have to sprout wings to transcend your surroundings.

The Field of Dreams. Tended to by the Gentle Gardener, the Field of Dreams is where you must go to plant your seeds of intent. Whatever you plant, she will help grow, so you must choose wisely. She will even ensure the integrity of poisonous plants.

The Field of Poppies. At first, this field of beautiful scarlet poppies seems delightful as it invites you to take a nap here . . . but beware. There is no restful, restorative sleep in the Field of Poppies, only a deep, narcotic slumber that will take you away from the experience of life. The lesson of this place is denial. You must wake up to gain the power of truth.

Flatville. In Flatville, the houses have but one "story" and are two-dimensional, as are the residents, who look like paper dolls. The landscape and people are flat because you land here when you oversimplify the narrative of your life and ignore the shadow and dark, the "dimension" to your experiences. This is a place where your prejudice takes root. The only way out is through accepting complexities.

The Frozen Land. When your emotional reality is so harsh that you shut down and become numb, you enter the Frozen Land, where time seems to stand still and the heat of your anger, fear, jealousy, or sadness is cooled. Here you can rest during a long winter's nap and dream new dreams for your life.

The Ghostlands. Whenever you're avoiding your emotions in the present, you find yourself in a Ghostland of nostalgia or regret, or wishful thinking or dread. You obsess about the past or future instead of dealing with today. A Ghostland may resemble any landscape, but its features (and *you*) are ethereal, because it is a place where no true emotion exists and therefore nothing can be learned or gained. You exit when you allow yourself to feel your difficult emotions.

The Golden Palace of Wealth on the Precipice. This luxurious castle is filled with material wealth and powerful, beautiful people who will befriend you, but even if you can persuade the snooty butler to let you past the velvet ropes, you'll find it a tantalizing and frustrating place. Touch the precious objects, fondle the gold bullion, and you'll feel the floor beneath you begin to give way: the palace teeters on the edge of a precipice, because material wealth is precarious. The real abundance here is in the garden, which you'll discover is the Field of Dreams.

The Immovable Mountain. When stuck at the base of the Immovable Mountain, exercise patience and look more closely at yourself, for you may discover you have the magical power to sprout wings, burrow through, or wind your way up the path until you arrive on the other side.

The Island of Broken Dreams. This place may resemble a junkyard, but when you look more closely, the frugal Bone Collector is standing over bones lost or never claimed. Their qualities are available to you at any time, should you choose to embrace them. Although the bones appear dry and brittle, the Bone Collector will gladly sing life into them; or burn them to ash that will fertilize what you plant in your Field of Dreams, thus allowing you to reclaim what was lost, just in a different form.

The Land of Unfairness. This is where the Ruthless Balancer lives, the force that strips away all but that which is completely necessary. Here you feel a sense of shock and betrayal as you recognize that things you felt entitled to are no longer yours. The hidden treasure in this place is the lesson that what you thought you couldn't live without wasn't necessary for your happiness after all, and joy is *always* available. The Land of Unfairness lies between the Valley of Loss and the Peaks of Joy.

Mount Hubris. Unlike the Immovable Mountain, which is one of the parameters on your map, Mount Hubris is an obstacle of your own making. You won't see it as a problem when you first approach it, because the mischievous Goblin knows how to hide its true nature from you. As it turns out, Mount Hubris isn't a mountain at all but merely a large hill, made up mostly of manure and bs.

The Peaks of Joy. These mountains are all over the Enchanted Map, always located on the borders of distressing landscapes, for you can't experience the indescribably wonderful Peaks of Joy unless you've visited the depths of despair and suffering.

The Raging River and the Wobbly Bridge. You may find yourself feeling forced downstream, desperately trying to keep your head above water in the Raging River. Or you might find yourself on its bank, calling in vain to someone you care about who is on the other side, in danger, but who can't hear you over the sound of the turbulent river. You may attempt to cross the Wobbly Bridge to rescue this person, but be careful, for the bridge might not hold and could send you into the waters below. Here you must learn the limitations of your ability to control all the details of your life and others' behavior.

The Resting Tree. At the base of the Resting Tree, you can take a break from the dramas and challenges of life. It will nurture you with vitality as you lean your back against its trunk, even as you nap. The Brownie at the Resting Tree is the Spirit of Place, and she can teach you the value of slowing down and becoming still and can reassure you that the world will get along just fine if you take a break.

Rock Bottom. Some people never reach Rock Bottom because they spend too much time in the Field of Poppies, avoiding their emotions, which is a shame because there are marvelous treasures here. At Rock Bottom, you awaken to the challenges you've been avoiding and finally learn the lesson of surrender. Here you discover the courage that comes from trusting in Spirit's plans for your life.

Shouldville. When obligations bombard you and you have difficulty setting firm boundaries with others, you find yourself in Shouldville. All the windows and doors of the houses are wide open, and you'll find that you're dressed in your pajamas as you walk down the street, trying to respond to all of the many obligations people impose upon you. You must set some boundaries with others in order to leave this distressing emotional landscape behind.

The Sticky Swamp. The air here is cloying and heavy, the muck beneath your feet a primordial ooze. Here you feel utterly stuck. If you relax and stop struggling, your feelings of being overwhelmed begin to subside, and you'll be able to move forward with creative ideas and clear priorities.

The Storm Fields. Anger and fear make the air crackle in the Storm Fields, where you must dodge lightning bolts as you run through the darkness, drenched by pouring rain. Find shelter, and discover your role in creating those lightning bolts that so frighten you. Then you'll learn to use your anger more productively—to spark new ideas, momentum, and impetus—and disengage from other people's angry dramas.

The Tranquil Lake. Rest at the Tranquil Lake, where the waters are so still that as you look at them, you can reflect upon your image and see your beauty. Around you the breezes are gentle, and the carpet of grass is soft beneath you. Here you may reflect, but you must also be willing to dive below the surface of these waters and look deeply into yourself with compassion. Otherwise, like Narcissus, you may become mesmerized by superficial thoughts about yourself that make you feel good.

The Valley of Loss. In this deep crevice in the land, you look up at hills that appear far too steep to climb and wonder how you'll ever escape to higher ground. You will have to return here at times even if you've fully learned the lesson of this place, because loss is a part of life.

The Vandalized House. You may find yourself here when your boundaries have been violated or disrespected, but also when you make choices that disrespect yourself, such as acting out in an addictive, compulsive way with respect to shopping, sex, drugs, alcohol, and so on. You live here when you believe your Home Tree has the word *victim* on the door. Instead of a chime, the door-bell rings: "Poor me, not enough, poor me." You're led here by the Goblin, who tricks you into believing this is your home. Yet the oracle is a tiny house elf who has a message for you: "You will never clean up this house until you accept where you are and take responsibility for your own healing." The minute you initiate a dialogue with the Goblin, he will fall fast asleep and you can begin getting out of here.

I'm sure you'll find other landscapes to explore, with *their* wise Spirits of Place. The most important gift in working with the Enchanted Map of You is discovery. Within you lies treasure that once found will reach into the world to find its counterpart in form.

May you be blessed on your journey.

Love,
Colette

BIBLIOGRAPHY

Armstrong, Karen. 2009. *The Case for God*. New York: Alfred A. Knopf.

Barber, Benjamin R. 2007. *Consumed*. New York: W. W. Norton & Co.

Braden, Gregg. 2008. *The Spontaneous Healing of Belief: Shattering the Paradigm of False Limits*. Carlsbad, California: Hay House.

———. 2009. *Fractal Time: The Secret of 2012 and a New World Age*. Carlsbad, California: Hay House.

Campbell, Joseph. 1988. *The Power of Myth*. New York: Anchor Books.

———. 2004. *Pathways to Bliss: Mythology and Personal Transformation*. Novato, California: New World Library.

———. 2008 (third edition). *The Hero with a Thousand Faces*. Novato, California: New World Library.

Dalai Lama, His Holiness the. 2005. *The Universe in a Single Atom: The Convergence of Science and Spirituality*. New York: Morgan Road Books.

Emoto, Masaru. 2005. *The Secret Life of Water*. New York: Atria Books.

Estés, Clarissa Pinkola, Ph.D. 1992. *Women Who Run with the Wolves: Myths and Stories of the Wild Woman Archetype*. New York: Ballantine Books.

Laszlo, Ervin, and Currivan, Jude. 2008. *CosMos: A Co-creator's Guide to the Whole-World*. Carlsbad, California: Hay House.

Lipton, Bruce, Ph.D. 2008. *The Biology of Belief: Unleashing the Power of Consciousness, Matter & Miracles*. Carlsbad, California: Hay House.

Lipton, Bruce, Ph.D., and Bhaerman, Steve. 2009. *Spontaneous Evolution: Our Positive Future (and a Way to Get There from Here)*. Carlsbad, California: Hay House.

Moore, Thomas; Dallaire, Roméo; Woodman, Marion; Lewis, Stephen; and Rutte,

Martin. 2006. *Seeking the Sacred: Leading a Spiritual Life in a Secular World.* Toronto: ECW Press.

Roszak, Theodore; Gomes, Mary E.; and Kanner, Allen D., eds. 1995. *Ecopsychology: Restoring the Earth, Healing the Mind.* San Francisco: Sierra Club Books.

Scott, Susan S. 2003. *Healing with Nature.* New York: Helios Press.

Shimoff, Marci. 2007. *Happy for No Reason: 7 Steps to Being Happy from the Inside Out.* New York: Free Press.

Starhawk. 2004. *The Earth Path: Grounding Your Spirit in the Rhythms of Nature.* San Francisco: HarperSanFrancisco.

ACKNOWLEDGMENTS

To my incredible, loving husband, Marc: Thank you for your patient support through all the versions of this book. You have shown me that indeed I was capable of planting great love in my Field of Dreams. I love you with all my heart and soul.

Thank you to Michelle Morgan for keeping the ship afloat and being such a wonderful and important part of the Too Amaze, Inc., family!

To my bundle of sparkles and joy, Michelle Grimm: Thank you for helping me midwife the content of this book through my intensives in Sedona. We've seen how it works. I couldn't have done it without you.

A humble thank-you to my editor Nancy Peske for saving this book from the Sticky Swamp and supporting my concepts and ideas so that they have clarity and authenticity. You work magic!

To Denise Linn, thank you for your wonderful, eloquent Foreword. I'm so grateful for your forever friendship and great guidance.

Thank you to Nancy Levin for allowing me to share your wonderful poetry. You are a true artist, and as you know, I'm your biggest fan!

Thank you to Courteney Cox Arquette for your support!

To Louise Hay: You totally rock, and I love you more than ice cream.

To Reid Tracy: Thanks for all the advice and guidance and patience and belief in me. Truly, you've changed my life. I am eternally grateful.

Thank you to Doug Upchurch for your loyal, caring guidance to show me that my work is to "show people how to find the magic and meaning in the story of their life!" And I'm deeply grateful for your help in showing me the "other book" needed to change.

Thank you to my dear darling soul sister Courtney Taylor for the years of support and friendship. To Nina and Dan, thank you for your unwavering hospitality, friendship, and support and family away from home.

To my longtime friend photographer and *artiste extraordinaire* Deborah Samuel, thank you for always bringing out the best of me.

To my friends and fellow authors Gregg Braden, Dr. Darren Weissman, and Dr. Bruce Lipton for the long, fabulous conversations and for your wonderful support of my work.

Thank you, also, to the most magical Jena DellaGrottaglia. *Wisdom of the Hidden Realms Oracle Cards* came alive through you, and I am ever so grateful that those wise beings called you back to me to create such an array of extraordinary inspired art for *The Enchanted Map of You Oracle Cards*.

Thank you to everyone at Hay House, Inc., and Hay House Radio who has touched my life and who makes it possible for my books and card decks to reach the world: Jill Kramer, Alex Freemon, Margarete Nielsen, Emily Manning, Diane Ray, Christa Gabler, Mollie Monday-Langer, Adrian Sandoval, Karen Stone, Matty, Aaron, Ram, everyone in customer service—and well, maybe I should just add the entire employee list here . . . I love you, Hay House!

Thank you, brilliant and dear Evelyn, for the countless hours of inspiring conversations. Although the "other book" wasn't meant to be, the quest led me to find treasure after all by discovering *The Map*.

And a million thanks to Jennifer Rudolph Walsh and Andy McNicol at WME.

ABOUT THE AUTHOR

Colette Baron-Reid is a popular intuitive counselor, psychic medium, seminar leader, radio personality, motivational speaker, best-selling author, and musical recording artist (with a top-selling meditation CD, *Journey Through the Chakras*). She currently lives in Sedona, Arizona, with her husband and their two furry children.

For information on seminars, intensives, and private sessions with Colette, as well as original meditation downloads to support your work with this book, visit: **www.colettebaronreid.com**.

NOTES

NOTES

NOTES

NOTES

Hay House Titles of Related Interest

YOU CAN HEAL YOUR LIFE, *the movie,*
starring Louise L. Hay & Friends
(available as a 1-DVD program and an expanded 2-DVD set)
Watch the trailer at: **www.LouiseHayMovie.com**

THE SHIFT, *the movie,*
starring Dr. Wayne W. Dyer
(available as a 1-DVD program and an expanded 2-DVD set)
Watch the trailer at: **www.DyerMovie.com**

THE ANGEL THERAPY® HANDBOOK, by Doreen Virtue

FRIED: Why You Burn Out and How to Revive,
by Joan Borysenko, Ph.D., with her Facebook Friends

HEALING YOUR FAMILY HISTORY: 5 Steps to Break Free
of Destructive Patterns, by Rebecca Linder Hintze

HOW TO FIND YOUR INNER PRIESTESS, by Kala Trobe

THE MOTHER OF INVENTION: The Legacy of Barbara Marx
Hubbard and the Future of YOU, by Neale Donald Walsch

THE NATURE OF INFINITE LOVE & GRATITUDE
Transformation Cards, by Dr. Darren R. Weissman

REPETITION: Past Lives, Life, and Rebirth,
by Doris Eliana Cohen, Ph.D.

TRANSFORMING FATE INTO DESTINY:
A New Dialogue with Your Soul, by Robert Ohotto

TRAVELING AT THE SPEED OF LOVE, by Sonia Choquette

All of the above are available at your local bookstore,
or may be ordered by contacting Hay House (see next page).

We hope you enjoyed this Hay House book.
If you'd like to receive our online catalog featuring
additional information on Hay House books and
products, or if you'd like to find out more about the
Hay Foundation, please contact:

Hay House, Inc., P.O. Box 5100, Carlsbad, CA 92018-5100
(760) 431-7695 or (800) 654-5126
(760) 431-6948 (fax) or (800) 650-5115 (fax)
www.hayhouse.com® • **www.hayfoundation.org**

Published and distributed in Australia by: Hay House Australia Pty. Ltd.,
18/36 Ralph St., Alexandria NSW 2015 • *Phone:* 612-9669-4299
Fax: 612-9669-4144 • www.hayhouse.com.au

Published and distributed in the United Kingdom by:
Hay House UK, Ltd., 292B Kensal Rd., London W10 5BE • *Phone:*
44-20-8962-1230 • *Fax:* 44-20-8962-1239 • www.hayhouse.co.uk

Published and distributed in the Republic of South Africa by:
Hay House SA (Pty), Ltd., P.O. Box 990, Witkoppen 2068
Phone/Fax: 27-11-467-8904 • www.hayhouse.co.za

Published in India by: Hay House Publishers India,
Muskaan Complex, Plot No. 3, B-2, Vasant Kunj, New Delhi 110 070
Phone: 91-11-4176-1620 • *Fax:* 91-11-4176-1630 • www.hayhouse.co.in

Distributed in Canada by: Raincoast,
9050 Shaughnessy St., Vancouver, B.C. V6P 6E5
Phone: (604) 323-7100 • *Fax:* (604) 323-2600 • www.raincoast.com

<u>Take Your Soul on a Vacation</u>

Visit **www.HealYourLife.com®** to regroup, recharge,
and reconnect with your own magnificence.
Featuring blogs, mind-body-spirit news, and
life-changing wisdom from Louise Hay and friends.

Visit **www.HealYourLife.com** today!